MOTHER TONGUE AND OTHER TONGUES

MOTHER TONGUE AND OTHER TONGUES
Narratives in Multilingual Psychotherapy

Edited by

Ali Zarbafi and Shula Wilson

PHOENIX
PUBLISHING HOUSE
firing the mind

First published in 2021 by
Phoenix Publishing House Ltd
62 Bucknell Road
Bicester
Oxfordshire OX26 2DS

British Library Cataloguing in Publication Data

A C.I.P. for this book is available from the British Library

ISBN-13: 978-1-912691-85-2

Typeset by Medlar Publishing Solutions Pvt Ltd, India

www.firingthemind.com

Contents

Acknowledgements

We would like to thank the contributors in this book for all the work and thought that has gone into creating the Multi-lingual Psychotherapy Centre and the work they have put into changing their talks into articles. We would like to thank Dr Judit Szekacs-Weisz who was one of the key founders of Imago-MLPC in 1998 and her contributions to the organisation and the field in general. We would like to thank Dr Laura Liverotti, Cédric Bouët-Willaumez, and Dr Esti Rimmer for reading some of the articles in this book and their thoughtful contributions. We would like to thank Svetlana Fleming and Orit Beck for the contributions they have made to the executive committee and lectures which undoubtedly are reflected in some of the thinking in this book. We would like to thank John Clare who for many years chaired our lectures and made many contributions in terms of writing and thinking to the multilingual project. Finally we would like to thank all those who attended the lectures and the profound contributions they made.

About the editors and contributors

Cédric Bouët-Willaumez is a psychotherapist and supervisor in private practice. An alumnus of HEC Business School in Paris, he had a first career in strategic consultancy before choosing to train as a psychotherapist. He graduated from the Centre for Counselling and Psychotherapy Education, London, in 2006. He worked for a number of charities as a frontline mental health worker and service manager, and was lead psychotherapist for a central London GP training practice between 2013 and 2018. He taught classes and led seminars in several psychotherapy training organisations, notably as part of the Multi-lingual Psychotherapy Centre, which he joined as a member in 2007, and then member of the executive committee in 2010.

Giselle China is a psychoanalytic psychotherapist in private practice, a training supervisor, and a musician. She grew up in Germany where she graduated in languages, linguistics, and philosophy. In England she taught languages initially, subsequently training as a counsellor and finally as a psychoanalytic psychotherapist. She is very interested in the issues of culture and language. She is a founder member of the Multi-lingual Psychotherapy Centre and a member of the executive.

Patricia Gorringe was born in Zimbabwe when it was a colony and grew up during the long civil war. She studied for her MPhil at the University of Cape Town and went on to pursue her PhD in the USA. She has lived in England since 1990 and worked in finance in the City of London for ten years. She qualified as a psychotherapist from Birkbeck College and has worked for an NHS-funded mental health organisation for fifteen years.

Natsu Hattori was born in Japan and moved with her parents to Canada. For the past twenty years she has lived mostly in England, with shorter periods in Brazil and Mexico. She has a background in languages and the arts and a PhD in English literature from Oxford University. She trained at the Gestalt Centre in London where she received an MA in Gestalt psychotherapy. She currently works as a psychotherapist in central and south-west London.

Monique Morris was born in Paris and came to live in London in her early twenties. Her professional background began in social work, where she worked in many settings such as child protection and mental health. She trained at the Guild of Psychotherapists and worked in private practice, the NHS, MIND, and Barnet Psychiatric Services.

Dr Esti Rimmer is a consultant clinical psychologist and a psychoanalytic psychotherapist. After studying psychology at the Hebrew University in Jerusalem, she received her doctorate in clinical psychology from the University of Denver, Colorado. She completed her psychoanalytic training at the Scottish Institute of Human Relations in Edinburgh, where she is currently director of training for the Scottish Association of Psychoanalytic Psychotherapy. She is now retired from the NHS in Northumberland, where she led a psychotherapy service and a mentoring programme for refugee health care workers, and is working in private practice.

Edna Sovin trained at Relate and the London Centre for Psychotherapy and is in private practice as an analytical psychotherapist and supervisor. As an only child she is particularly interested in sibling relationships and how these are experienced in the transference in therapy.

Shula Wilson has been a practising psychotherapist and supervisor since 1991. She was the founder of SKYLARK (1995–2012) an organisation that offered counselling and psychotherapy for people affected by disability. She is a founder member of the Institute for Psychotherapy and Disability, and a consultant psychotherapist at St Thomas' Hospital and Great Ormond Street Hospital, where she is also a lecturer and supervisor. She is a committee member of the Multi-lingual Psychotherapy Centre. Shula is the author of *Disability, Counselling and Psychotherapy—Challenges and Opportunities* (Palgrave Macmillan, 2003) and has written chapters and articles on disability and psychotherapy for various publications.

Dr Ali Zarbafi is an Anglo-Iranian Jungian analyst and supervisor and member of the Society of Analytical Psychology with thirty years' clinical experience. He is a founder member of the Multi-lingual Psychotherapy Centre. Ali works in the NHS and private practice. He has written and given talks on trauma, the refugee experience, and social dreaming, and has an academic background in international relations and Middle Eastern studies. He has co-written a book with John Clare, *Social Dreaming in the 21st Century: The World We Are Losing* (Karnac, 2009).

Introduction

Ali Zarbafi

All cultures are concerned with how we speak and communicate as this represents identity, history, and home. Communication is also essential for survival, emotionally and socially. The way we speak is a communication of care, concern, empathy, or distance and indifference. It is also a communication of a country, a region, a class, and an experience. Speaking a language is an emotional experience; it is very loaded and full of pleasure and pain. The speaking person is both an individual and part of a culture, or cultures, with dense collective and individual shapes. We are always faced with finding out about each other as well as hoping that we share similar assumptions. The issue of identity, which is a feeling of belonging, is essential, full of possibility and sometimes very uncomfortable as it touches the tensions between who we are and who we are becoming. This simple everyday sentiment sits next to more complex historical experiences and memories of languages and cultures being changed or lost or banished due to the colonial, imperial, and regional moves of powerful nations in search of conquest and economic gain.

We are now living in times where the issue of identity and difference has taken on a more defensive hue. The tide is turning towards an inward looking nostalgia of sameness based on fear rather than understanding. The experience of hearing another language, the way it is spoken. and being faced with the image of the other is now more complex as it is imbued with projections of powerlessness, fear, terrorism, and survival. This is also because the so-called native speaker, especially in the Western world, has lost confidence in who they actually are historically and how they can speak from where they come from with some perspective. This is in part due to a world in which national and regional identities and communities are secondary to transnational politics and economics, and so the psychological consequences for national and regional communities are those of fear and feeling forgotten, which leads to a return to an imagined or idealised past.

Houses in search of a home

The Multi-lingual Psychotherapy Centre emerged in the 1990s out of a need to mine the creativity of multiculturalism and difference from a group of psychotherapists who came together weekly to read psychoanalytic papers. This group was ongoing for five years and eventually formed Imago-MLPC as it became clear that there was a common theme in the group related to being international both culturally and linguistically. Gradually a recurring theme began to emerge, not related to the psychoanalytic studies, posing the question of our identity; the group's identity. So we embarked on a social dreaming session. Social dreaming (Lawrence, 1998) is a method which allows individuals in a group called a matrix, within a certain time frame, to bring dreams and associations to the dreams. The dreams are seen as material thrown up from the human social world, rather than belonging to an individual dreamer and so can create new associations, conversations, and further dreams without the need to analyse or get anywhere. Social dreaming is about the centrality of the social world in the dreaming individual. Dreams do not "belong" to the individual. They are relational, with the other in mind. This method used in any group or organisational context tends to illuminate unconscious preoccupations not available on a more conscious thinking level.

The most powerful result of those sessions was that we all dreamt of houses: houses made of cardboard, corner houses, inside-out houses, back-to-front houses, houses that were split … houses in search of a home, a joint home, a common home, a shared home? Dreaming together was a turning point, as at that point we became a set of individuals who were dreaming about finding ourselves together in London but from different parts of the world. What sort of house was this that we were unconsciously sharing and living in? This house was obviously one of cultural and linguistic diversity, of immigration and emigration, of being lost and being found, of difference and otherness.

Our inaugural lecture entitled "Displacement: Psychotherapy in my father's language" was given in December 1997. The series that followed became known as the Burgh House Lectures. We have had forty lectures since the first and organised three conferences in the last twenty years, and published a book (Szekacs-Weisz & Ward, 2004).

Our aim, initially ambitious, became modest in time with three lectures a year and a conference possibly every three to four years, as we are a skeletal executive committee doing this work voluntarily and always looking for new members. The executive committee is made up of psychoanalytic, Jungian, and integrative psychotherapists. Our meetings are always interesting as we are constantly remembering or discussing an aspect of the multilingual experience either in our clinical work or in culture, that is, films, plays, politics, and everyday happenings. The lectures over the years have thrown up many ideas and thoughts. The speakers are invited to share their experience and the audience to free associate and there is a general atmosphere of sharing and remembering, a semblance of home.

Some ideas and thoughts that emerged through the years

a. How do we experience and use our mother tongue when we are living in a second learnt language? What happens to it and how does it affect our learning of a second language? Is our emotional compass always in our original language? How do we think about this clinically?
b. What is the relationship between your clinical language and your original language, which may be different? How is intimacy spoken or represented in different languages?

c. What do we do when there are no words in the new language, which we can easily find in our mother tongue? Are we faced with loss, limitation, creativity, or just an awareness of being outside?

d. How do we live "in-between" languages, betwixt and between as one speaker put it? Neither here nor there, always between, always moving where there is no sense of belonging.

e. Where is the language of the father and how is it different from the mother's language? What happens to a child who lives in father's country but has a mother who speaks a foreign language? What is this like for the child who learns the language of the father's culture as a first language as she or he grows up?

f. One speaker wondered why it was so easy to swear in a learnt second language and how difficult it was to swear in the mother tongue. Somehow the second language freed her up but was it that easy or was it to do with a lack of emotional attachment?

g. Others spoke of how the mother tongue was the forbidden language, or the language they needed to get away from, as it was too limiting, or painful. They put themselves in exile but somehow still carried this with them and needed ultimately to return to and think about their own exile. Yet others spoke of feeling exiled in their own countries by having to adopt the language of the coloniser which was at odds with their cultural experience, distorting and disturbing their sense of control and meaning.

h. Maybe exile provides new possibilities unavailable in your original country and emotional language. Maybe it offers you perspective and an ability to think about your emotional life.

i. And yet there was always a thought that culture and language precedes us for many generations. We carry the emotional atmosphere of our culture of birth throughout our lives even though we move away and build new lives and create new cultures and learn and create new languages. Our generational heritage always accompanies us in our new perspective and learning and never actually leaves us despite our best efforts. This can sometimes be represented by the accent which has an emotional hue. Somehow words are only traces of something much more—a collective home that we know about in our cultural histories and to which we add, even though we may not be able to put it into words too clearly.

Language, culture, and exile

Marcello Vinar, a Latin American psychoanalyst speaking from Paris while in exile from Argentina says,

> To speak in a language implies the knowledge of more than words but other things as well about the culture that produces it. One might be able to understand the dictionary and at the same time not know much at all. Alienation comes from not being able to interpret the meaning of the words but much, even more importantly, the meaning of gestures, references and social relations. It is an unforgettable experience … (Hollander, 1998, p. 209)

This "unforgettable experience" is emotional and linked to how the mother interprets culturally the intimate space for the child, initially through sounds and gestures ("motherese") which are accompanied by words, which the child starts finding after the age of one (Stern, 1985). The intimate space will be imbued with the cultural codes and fantasies about childhood and motherhood, which will have its limits and truths (Maitra & Krause, 2015). This is the seat of identity and the self, from which the child/adult will be able to read his or her world, which will be within a culture, but also be able to tolerate and be curious about difference, that is, other cultures through a collective notion of being human (Papadopoulos, 2002). The child will be able to develop a reflective ability where affect can be recognised as feelings and then made sense of by thoughts and words, and, by becoming aware of other minds, develop an ethical sense of right and wrong (Fonagy et al., 2004).

Exile from this cultural home is the beginning of a journey and immediately faces us with a loss of identity and an impoverishment of the feeling self, and an awareness of what we have taken for granted which is generally vast. There is trauma and alienation in this journey but also a need to survive which can promise renewal. The need to survive involves learning a new language in order to gain some control and power in the new culture. Some learn quickly to survive, to perhaps forget or park the trauma and find a new identity as soon as possible. Others learn very slowly as there is a resistance and guilt at betraying the mother tongue and culture (Hollander, 1998, p. 209). Others are unable to learn a second language as they are emotionally frozen and unable to break out of feelings of terror, shock, and guilt until there is some form of empathic understanding of their feelings in the mother tongue (Zarbafi, 2020).

The second language offers a life raft to the psyche as it involves a form of distancing from the mother tongue which can be creative as it affords perspective and recovery. For some this life raft is a getting away from a toxic mother tongue, others will use it instrumentally to survive, whereas others will find a more comfortable bridge to the second language if their mother tongue was a good enough seat of identity and reflective capacity. Bollas (1978), speaking about our relationship to the language of the mother says:

> If failure occurs, let us say, at the point of acquiring the Word, the Word may become a meaningless expression of the child's internal world. Words may feel useless, or, if the rules of the family prohibit words that speak the mood of the self, they may feel dangerous. (p. 390)

How one acquires the mother tongue, which has a cultural location, affects how one may experience a second language as well. Clare (2004) makes this point very well when discussing Beckett. Clare argues that Beckett needed to leave Ireland and his mother tongue in order to gain some much-needed distance from his mother. He went to Paris after a short analysis with Bion in London. It was only by gaining this distance that Beckett was able to write more than twenty pieces or books in French and then retranslate himself back into English. French was a form of life raft in which his unconscious could be explored before he could express himself more freely and clearly in his mother tongue.

Other writers such as Tesone (1996) and Antinucci-Mark (1990) elaborate this point about how the second language distances us from the overwhelming mother tongue. Tesone, an Italian analyst and Freudian, compares the use and learning of a second language which comes after the original mother tongue as a sort of detour and distance from the affect-ridden mother tongue. In looking at a detailed case study Tesone points out that the foreign language his patient used was "representative" and therefore carried an ambiguous connection to the overloaded mother tongue. The ambivalence enabled distance and perspective.

Antinucci-Mark hints at the inter-lingual space which exists between languages and in therapy, back and forth, which is enriching and new for both, and which is my experience of languages.

Clinically it is crucial to understand how language functions in the consulting room and this is generally available through one's counter-transference, as well as other clues such as how easily the patient may say something in the second language, which may feel inappropriate or at odds with what the therapist is feeling or lack the appropriate affect.

This is rather like Ferenczi's (Dupont, 1988) point about the difficulty of swearing in the original language. The second language enables clearer and more honest communication as it does not carry the emotional depth and consequences of the first language.

Language however, exists in a cultural context. The innatist view of language was put forward by Chomsky in 1957 in which he proclaims that we have a language gene and below all languages there is a universal grammar. This has been under serious question for many years (Everett, 2017). Chomsky's is still the dominant view which presumably also influences psychological and psychoanalytic theories where culture is always seen as secondary to the psyche, which Stolorow and Atwood (1992) call "the myth of the isolated mind" proclaimed by drive theory and object relations theory (Stolorow & Atwood, 1992, p. 7). The mind is social and cultural and always exists in relation to an "other" or a group and so is part of a larger cultural context (Coleman, 2013). For Chomsky, language is the same everywhere ultimately, whatever the culture (Deutscher, 2011). Obviously psyche and language exist everywhere but the point is that these deep parts of ourselves exist within, and informed by, a broader cultural context which shapes and limits what can and cannot be said or represented in words, or what can and cannot be thought and felt (Everett, 2017).

Cultures are transgenerational and emerge as systems of meaning to make sense of a particular environment, context, and history and so will have nuanced complexities. Language is a necessary and subtle system of communication to do with survival between self and other (Lichtenberg, Lackmann, & Fosshage, 2002). This system of communication exists in a cultural home, which has a past, a present, and a future (Papadopoulos, 2002). The idea that somehow language or psyche are pure structures and that culture is secondary has traces of a colonial and orientalist view of culture which is seen to belong to "others" and is not of any real value (Said, 1978). In the West we are keenly aware of this even in the way English, for example, is spoken and felt in the UK or the United States or Australia. It is the same language but affected deeply in meaning and use by the cultural context which is historical. As Durkheim puts it, "Language is a product of collective elaboration. What it expresses is the manner in which society as a whole represents the facts of experience" (Lander, 1966, p. 149).

Contributors to this book

The theme of culture, language, and exile and the internal and external journeys taken is traversed in all the chapters in this book through personal narratives, literature, film, and clinical thinking and vignettes. The authors, who are all psychotherapists, have had to think about internal homes, external homes, and new homes, represented by a variety of languages, senses, and places and how this has impacted on their work. There is a sense of resilience which comes through these chapters in the authors' attempts to reflect and make sense of their journeys away from home and back again and how this has impacted and created new identities, languages, and senses of self.

The chapters track journeys from Germany, Israel, France, Japan, Zimbabwe, and Iran to countries in the West—England, the USA, and Canada. All have their nuances and shapes, with some being enforced exiles and others being exiles by choice through getting away from toxic experiences.

In our first chapter Esti Rimmer, having initially left Israel for the USA, thoughtfully explores the meaning of internal and external exile through stories and literature, clinical thinking and vignettes. Using the phrase "the uncanny" and the image of the fish caught in the sands who manages to survive, she explores exile as the wish to forget and the fear of forgetting.

In the second chapter Ali Zarbafi explores his journey of exile from his English mother tongue to Iran, the language of his father, and back again. Working with a childhood nightmare, Ali adopts the idea of writing out his nightmare into many languages, that is, dreaming, politics, psychotherapy, and the refugee experience, to create meaning out of his journey of exile and living in between languages.

Natsu Hattori movingly speaks of her loss of her Japanese language and culture in the new world of Canada where Japanese was spoken inside and English outside. Where faced with being metaphorically deaf in English when she first arrived, she learnt to speak the English language eloquently, culminating in a PhD in English literature, but somehow felt illiterate and young in Japanese. Natsu uses stories and clinical thinking and vignettes to illustrate her journey.

Patricia Gorringe, in contrast, discusses the lack of comfort and meaning in the second language and the importance of the physical as a language of communication when there is no second language to learn. Having to flee from Zimbabwe where she spoke English, she found the English language in the USA barren. She was faced with the terror of speaking and she explores the importance of this experience through clinical thinking and detailed clinical vignettes with two patients.

Monique Morris discusses her accents in her generational story of loss and abandonment from Algeria to a grim post-war Paris to London, where she ponders her identity and how her French accent eventually faces her with her roots and need for a new identity. She offers a thoughtful meditation on the meaning of Pygmalion, being French in England, and her return to France and how her accent meant that she belonged to both and neither.

Cédric Bouët-Willaumez, having left France, speaks eloquently about his internal conversation between his Dutch mother tongue, his French father tongue, and his other more liberating tongues of English and music. Charting his inner journey, from a research project with psychotherapists, his readings, and his clinical work, he discusses Abdallah, a character in *Tintin* who has great power and wealth yet is motherless. He suggests that a new language is a new representation of mother.

The theme of discarded languages is continued by Edna Sovin where she explores her relationship to German. Edna was born of a German Jewish family and came to England before the war at a very young age. Speaking German with her parents was taboo and shameful and so she learnt English and was unaware of her extended family until later on in her life when she returned to Germany to speak of her feminist grandmother who she discovered through letters.

Giselle China continues this theme of shame around the German language and how she disavowed it when she moved to England. Her English voice allowed her to speak and transform her sense of silence around being German. She describes English as a language she was reborn in, the language of life and not death, and goes on to describe the wound of silence surrounding being a second-generation German and not wanting to look back to Germany in a horrifying historical period.

The final chapter in the book fittingly returns to the theme of home by Shula Wilson. Shula explores the meaning of home as an idea and in Hebrew as an internal and external space which has intimacy, feeling, and belonging in it. The lack of this internal feeling of a secure space can lead to a search for home which she illustrates with a clinical vignette. Finding home is something we do when we are witnessed and feel met by the other, and in this way we can feel part of a culture and a language where we can start to reflect on our life and journey.

One of the themes that emerged out of all the talks on which these contributions were based was the importance of the discussion after the talk, where the multicultural and accented audience discussed their own journeys, cultures, and languages. The language of psychotherapy was only one language in the room which enabled thinking, but it was also being culturally informed by the different ways in which we can translate ourselves internally and externally. It was an enriching, open, and generous experience not framed or dominated by any one language of understanding. The speaker was only one storyteller in a room surrounded by many stories rich in feelings informed by generational histories, of not knowing and discovery.

As you read this book you are invited to engage with the tradition of our lectures, where the papers—now the chapters—can be read as stand-alone reflections, memories, and stories which in themselves give a glimpse of the multilingual journey we have been exploring for over twenty years.

References

Antinucci-Mark, G. (1990). Speaking in tongues in the consulting room or the dialectics of foreignness. *British Journal of Psychotherapy*, 6(4): 375–383.

Bollas, C. (1978). The aesthetic moment and the search for transformation. *The Annual of Psychoanalysis*, 6: 385–394.

Chomsky, N. (1957). *Syntactic Structures*. The Hague, the Netherlands: Mouton de Gruyter.

Clare, J. (2004). Getting away from the mother tongue: Samuel Beckett and psychoanalysis. In: J. Szekacs-Weisz & I. Ward (Eds.), *Lost Childhood and the Language of Exile* (pp. 182–192). London: The Freud Museum.

Coleman, W. (2013). Bringing it all back home: How I became a relational analyst. *Journal of Analytical Psychology*, 58(4): 470–490.

Deutscher, G. (2011). *Through the Language Glass: Why the World Looks Different in Other Languages*. London: Arrow.

Dupont, J. (Ed.) (1988). *The Clinical Diary of Sándor Ferenczi*. Cambridge, MA: Harvard University Press.

Everett, D. (2017). *How Language Began*. London: Profile.

Fonagy, P., Gergely, G., Jurist, E., & Target, M. (Eds.) (2004). *Affect Regulation, Mentalization, and the Development of the Self*. London: Karnac.

Hollander, N. C. (1998). Exile: Paradoxes of loss and creativity. *British Journal of Psychotherapy*, 15(2): 201–215.

Lander, H. (1966). *Language and Culture*. Oxford: Oxford University Press.

Lawrence, W. G. (Ed.) (1998). *Social Dreaming @ Work*. London: Karnac.

Lichtenberg, J. D., Lackmann, F. M., & Fosshage, J. L. (Eds.) (2002). *A Spirit of Enquiry: Communication in Psychoanalysis*. Hillsdale, NJ: Analytic Press.

Maitra, B., & Krause, I.-B. (Eds.) (2015). *Culture and Madness*. London: Jessica Kingsley.

Papadopoulos, R. K. (2002). *Therapeutic Care for Refugees: No Place Like Home*. London: Karnac.

Said, E. W. (1978). *Orientalism*. London: Routledge & Kegan Paul.

Stern, D. N. (1985). *The Interpersonal World of the Infant*. New York: Basic Books.

Stolorow, R. D., & Atwood, G. E. (1992). *Contexts of Being. The Intersubjective Foundations of Psychological Life*. Hillsdale, NJ: Analytic Press.

Szekacs-Weisz, J., & Ward, I. (Eds.) (2004). *Lost Childhood and the Language of Exile*. London: Karnac.

Tesone, J. (1996). Multi-lingualism, word-presentations, thing-presentations and psychic reality. *International Journal of Psychoanalysis*, 77: 871–881.

Zarbafi, A. (2020). Language, politics and dreams: The challenge of building resilience in refugees. *Journal of Analytical Psychology*, 65(2): 281–299.

CHAPTER ONE

Language of the mountains, language of the sea: living with exile and trauma as a journey between languages

Esti Rimmer

"We have already often observed that every time an author confronts the subject of multilingualism within the dimension of the psychoanalytic rapport, he inevitably ends up talking about himself" (Amati-Mehler, Argentieri, & Canestri, 1993). This observation is shared by Miletic (2008), who suggests that "linguistic migration and any other form of multilingualism is a highly personal experience" (p. 16).

These reflect my sentiments exactly, so in order to avoid the trap of eventually talking about myself, I will immediately do so by recounting a dream. I had this dream when I was about nine years old while visiting Jerusalem with my parents and sister from the small seaside town where I grew up. We were travelling to see my brother, who had just begun reading psychology at the Hebrew University in Jerusalem. He was living in an old house, in a neighbourhood close to the university that had been largely settled by German-Jewish immigrants. The house belonged to Frau Prof Brachyahu, who rented rooms to students. My brother explained to me that she was the widow of Prof Brachyahu, the man who had translated Freud into Hebrew. He even showed me his copy of *The Interpretation of Dreams* and explained about Freud and psychoanalysis.

That night I was invited to stay over at my brother's house—my parents and sister were staying elsewhere. I slept on the little living room couch, which felt like an exciting adventure. As night fell and the big house became dark and full of unfamiliar sounds, I felt a bit frightened. In my dream, one of the many doors along the hallway creaked open and a light appeared underneath. Suddenly, two older men appeared, who seemed to be conversing in German, a language I was used to hearing, since, although between themselves my parents spoke Hungarian, they had many friends with whom they spoke German. At this point in the dream, I grew frightened and tried to hide under the covers, not to be spotted, but when they walked past the couch, one of the men noticed me. He turned and asked me brusquely in Hebrew: "What are you doing here, little girl?" The other man, whom I took to be Freud, turned to me, smiled, and said in perfect Hebrew: "Oh, leave her alone, she is not disturbing us. You can go back to sleep, little girl."

A few months after that night my father died. My mother, who always pined for the Carpathian Mountains of her childhood, decided to move our family from the small seaside town to Jerusalem, which is nestled in the mountains. Thus began my first internal exile, from the sea to the mountains, which would be followed by several others in later life.

Trauma and exile

In this chapter, I would like to draw on clinical vignettes and an example from literature to reflect on the effects of trauma and exile and the migration between languages, as they might play out in the therapeutic encounter. Yet the more I considered these concepts in my attempts to integrate them into a coherent narrative, the more slippery they became. I have thus come to realise that primary processes play an important part in thinking about the languages of trauma and exile. Hence this text is fashioned from reflections, fragments, memories, images, and vignettes, which will hopefully fire the reader's own imagination and processes of thought, rather than provide clear answers.

It seems apparent that trauma and exile are intimately linked. The physical act of exile—the movement from one geographical location to another under duress, or in order to survive—tends to follow some degree of trauma, such as war or persecution. Furthermore, the mere process of migration carries with it the trauma of an interrupted life, the disconnection from the previous location, and the lack of connection, at the beginning, to new, alien surroundings. Thus, exile oscillates between at least two major traumas. In parallel, following a traumatic event, which may not necessarily involve physical migration, there is also a process of exile. In this case, though, it is an internal exile: a migration from a pre-traumatic internal space to a post-traumatic internal space, which may feel foreign or uncanny (*unheimlich*). In short, a psychic exile.

Trauma, then, involves a form of exile, as much as exile involves trauma. Indeed, every separation entails a sense of rupture and loss (Winnicott, 1982). There is a difference, however, between the experience of separation and loss as part of a normal developmental process and that which occurs in exile. Whereas normal separation is driven by a positive maturational process, as the child gradually increases a sense of autonomy in the world, exile is perceived to be a forceful removal, an unnatural interruption of the connectedness between a person and a specific time and place. This feeling of the uncanny is beautifully expressed by the words of Gholam Husain Sa'edi (1986), an Iranian writer in exile in Paris:

> It is now nearly two years since I have become a refugee in this place, spending every few nights in a friend's house. I feel uprooted. Nothing seems real. Paris buildings all seem like theatrical set pieces. I imagine I am living inside a postal card. I fear two things: one is sleeping, the other is waking. (p. 4)

Exile may be forced by external events, or internally compelled, but in both cases may be perceived as an external force which has ruptured the natural flow of things; feeling plucked from one's natural environment to be transplanted elsewhere.

In his essay, "Writing in Tongues", the exiled Turkish writer Moris Farhi, who writes in English, talks about the concept of the *insabbiati*. The word refers to fish caught in the sand and was coined for those Italians with colonial dreams who, having participated in Mussolini's invasion of Ethiopia in 1936, chose to stay on after Italy's defeat at the end of World War II. Farhi uses the image of the fish caught in the sand to refer to "the other": exiles, refugees, immigrants, displaced people, outsiders, outcasts. He goes on to describe the *insabbiati* as:

> a creature neither quite dead nor quite alive; a creature that could not adapt to its native matrix—or never got the chance to do so—yet one that managed to survive, sometimes even thrive, in unknown outlandish environments. Indubitably, an ancient species with genes that must still be the envy of chameleons. (Farhi, 2001, p. 128)

Hamid Naficy (1993), an Iranian academic in exile, highlights the paradox of exile. He points out that:

> While most definitions of exile consider it to be a dystopic and dysphoric experience stemming from deprivation, exile must also be defined by its utopian and euphoric possibilities, driven by wanderlust and a desire for liberation and freedom. (p. 6)

As trauma involves some form of exile—internal or external—so exile involves some form of trauma—a rupture. In her paper, "Thinking about Trauma", Garland (2017) talks about the collapse of meaning that accompanies the experience of trauma, as well as the breakdown of the smooth running of the mind's defensive structure and the loss of the belief in the protection afforded by good objects.

When Ferenczi (1933) spoke about the confusion of tongues in his study of sexual trauma in childhood, he meant of course the child's confusion between the language of affection and the language of desire. However, I would like to suggest that every trauma creates a confusion of tongues. It is the confusion between the mother tongue—the language of affection—and the language of horror. Trauma and migration involve a rupture, albeit temporary, between words and meaning; or, as Eva Hoffman (2008) suggests, the dissociation between the object and its signifier. In both cases there is a break in the narrative: a rupture in what is known, familiar, construed, and understood, sometimes to the point where there are no words left in any language.

In describing exile, Naficy employs the metaphor of a lift, which he borrows from his own dream to describe what he calls the stage of liminality—defined by the Collins English Dictionary as relating to a point or a threshold beyond which a sensation becomes too faint to experience—of being stuck in-between, on the threshold of, in transition from a past life to a new one. Naficy (1993) states:

> As a metaphor, this image of ambivalence provokes several questions: Is a person in exile entitled to a piece of land as small as an elevator/ Is he condemned to travel up and down in it between two cultural poles, two memories, two lives? Is there a third in between zone or territory that is safe from both/ Is exile merely a claustrophobic space that provides shelter and acts like a prison, or is it a liberatory slip zone of possibilities and potentialities? (p. 13)

One cannot discuss a transitional space like the metaphor of the lift without thinking about Winnicott's transitional space and phenomena. Winnicott (1982) refers to the transitional object as that which enables the child to make the transition from the primary caregiver to developing relationships with others. The transitional object allows the individual to start the process of separation with the comfort of the illusion that the object offers. In other words, they can always carry with them something of importance: a neutral area of experience that will not be challenged (Laplanche & Pontalis, 1967).

Like the lift, this transitional space is neither internal, nor external, reality. Rather, it is an illusionary space in-between, an intermediate space where creativity, imagination, and transformation can take place. As in the case of the developing infant, there is a parallel to be drawn for all phenomena of transition and in particular that of exile, where language migration takes place in the realm of the transitional space between languages and cultures.

Migrating to another language

In thinking about how language migration might play a part in the elaboration of trauma and exile, I would like to use the example of a novel written by Aharon Appelfeld, an Israeli author. *The Man Who Never Stopped Sleeping* (2017) is a semi-autobiographical book which describes the journey of a young refugee boy from Bukovina, a German-speaking region of Romania in the Carpathian Mountains, to his early years in Palestine/Israel after the Second World War. Aaron Irvin was ten at the outbreak of war. Prior to the deportation of his Jewish parents to a concentration camp, his father had entrusted him to the care of a local farmer who kept him in hiding.

Following several years of hard labour, near starvation, and being hidden in the farmer's basement, the boy escapes and hides in the forests until the end of the war. He is found by other refugees who carry him with them to the displaced people's camp in Italy, where he joins other young refugees in preparation for illegal immigration to Palestine. Unlike the other boys, however, he spends most of his time sleeping, to such an extent that he has to be literally carried by the group on various legs of the journey. In his sleep he dreams about his parents, in their home. He speaks to them in German. They mention the war and acknowledge that they had been apart, yet, paradoxically, they are just the same, engaged in the same activities. His mother makes her usual delicacies and his father is at his desk writing. The boy lives in a parallel universe. In his sleep, he is in Bukovina, as though nothing has changed. Awake, he notices he is on the beach near Naples and the light hurts his eyes. While the other survivors are busy reconstructing their lives, he sleeps on. He says, "In sleep I was connected, with no barrier, to my parents and to the house where I grew up, and I continued to live my life and theirs" (Appelfeld, 2017, p. 13).

Garland (2017) talks about the extreme defensive measures of the ego following trauma, to the point of denial. In Irvin's case he maintains the illusion, in his sleeping state and through his dreams, that no rupture has taken place. While asleep, he is back home. Yet Irvin slowly begins to engage with the reality of life around him. He takes part in the training regime set up by Ephraim, the youth worker sent by the kibbutz to prepare him for his new life. This regime comprises physical exercises to get him stronger and fitter and is intended to prepare him for life on a kibbutz. Simultaneously, he is taught a new language: Hebrew. Ephraim forces the boys to speak only Hebrew and they are given new Hebrew names: Irvin becomes Aaron.

Irvin/Aaron describes his struggles with the new language, which was completely alien to him. Here is his description of the migration to this new language, which was an *unheimlich* experience:

> After morning line-up, we would go out for a run. "Alef is ohel, ohel is 'tent'," we shouted. "Beit is bayit, bayit is 'house'; gimel is

gag, gag is 'roof'; dalet is delet, delet is 'door'; heh is har, har is 'mountain.'" Every morning we added new words. The words I learned on that seashore were linked to the sea in my mind [...]. The sea was so intense that every new word was filled with its blue water and tempered in the burning light of the sun.

One evening Ephraim spoke again about the need to attach our language to our bodies. Every Hebrew word added strength. I didn't understand how words became connected to the body, but Ephraim's words seemed like correct instructions. If we listened to them, we would grow properly, and our thinking would be orderly and clear.

Slowly, imperceptibly, we distanced ourselves from everything that had been in us: the ghetto, the hiding places, the forests. From the southern coast of Naples, they seemed distant and blurry, as if they had lost their dreadful immediacy. (Appelfeld, 2017, pp. 19–20)

However, this newfound respite in the new language starts to create a conflict for Aaron. Again he dreams of his mother, but this time he is unable to speak to her. After a long silence he is only able to say one word: "mother". His mother seems so happy to hear this word and attempts to continue the conversation. He is finally able to tell her that he has a new language: "It was the language of the sea [...] with all the colours and smells of the sea." His mother becomes increasingly perplexed and upset: "Won't you cultivate your mother tongue anymore?" He tries to reassure her that the language of the sea may be a strong one but the mother tongue is stronger, but she is not convinced. The dream ends with his mother pleading with him not to replace their language with one she can't understand.

The dream evokes Aaron's guilt about betraying his mother. In adopting another language, it is as if he has taken a new love object. An oedipal struggle emerges, which sets up a triangle between him, his mother tongue, and his new tongue. This stirs up the fear of loss and retaliation: fear of losing the capacity to remember his mother, to communicate with her. The paradox of exile and trauma is expressed in these two opposing poles—the wish to forget and the fear of forgetting. This conflict is re-enacted as the internal struggle between the languages. Nevertheless, Irvin/Aaron starts to engage with his new life and begins to make new friends in the kibbutz, all immigrants like him. Yet he admires his friend Marek who refuses to change his name.

His adjustment is cut short, however, when he is sent to fight and is severely injured in his first battle. He spends months in hospital and undergoes multiple operations. In hospital he can sleep again and dreams of his parents but suffers intense physical pain and his sleep is disturbed. This time there is more conflict and transformation. He dreams of coming home and not being remembered. Life continues without him. Everything is the same but he no longer belongs. He then asks the staff and other patients to find him the last book he read before his family was deported: *Siddhartha* by Herman Hesse. He asks for the German copy, which is nowhere to be found. He says he needs the book the way he needs air to breathe. This is a search for the transitional object, which may help him hold on to the illusion of no separation and loss.

Naficy (1993) speaks about the fetishisation of narratives, images, symbols, and cultural products from the home country as playing a significant role in exile cultures. This heightened emotional attachment, to the point of an almost sacred devotion to the "fetishes", the frozen relics of the home country, helps control the terror and chaos in this transitional stage, similar to Winnicott's (1982) idea of the transitional object. Eventually, Aaron settles on another sacred relic: the Bible. He starts learning Hebrew by copying the Bible word for word, trying to link words to their meanings. It is not until he talks to the kind, German-speaking Dr Winter, who speaks to him in his mother's German, that he starts crying and is able to make some link between words, meanings, and feelings.

Finding meaning: clinical vignettes

Chaim

This episode in Aaron's story resonates with my own clinical experience with a patient, who I shall call Chaim. (In Hebrew Chaim means life.) In my earlier days as a trainee clinical psychologist, I worked in a hospital on the East Coast of America. Chaim was brought in by the police and admitted under a mental health section due to a suicide risk. Chaim was a wealthy businessman in his early fifties, married with three children.

In his early twenties, following his recovery from an injury in the Israeli army, he emigrated to America and made his fortune. But his business had suffered due to the recession and he was about to become bankrupt. From a phone booth, he phoned his Israeli friends on the West Coast to say goodbye and to tell them of his plan to drive off a bridge. He made sure his family would be well looked after financially by various policies, but he had wanted his friends to know of his plan. In what sounds like a very dramatic and heroic plan, his friends contacted the police, who traced the phone booth, picked him up, and brought him to the hospital.

On admittance he appeared very calm and rational and showed no sign of distress. There was no evidence of psychosis or clinical depression. He engaged with life in the unit, ate and slept well. He was very polite but made it clear there was nothing wrong with him and that his was a logical solution: once he was discharged he would kill himself. He refused to see his family. Every attempt to engage him by the staff resulted in the same conversation: curt polite answers, no emotion, only logical, calculated, and well-articulated arguments. Eventually, the senior psychologist who supervised me asked me to see him. She said I came from the same place and perhaps I could get through to him. I felt indignant and resentful. I questioned why it should matter that we shared a mother tongue. He spoke perfectly good English, after almost thirty years in the country, while my English was good enough, so what would be the point?

Moreover, I felt awkward using a language other than English in this very New England, WASP establishment. I also did not like being associated with him as I found him distant and arrogant. A trainee doesn't have much choice, though. So I went to see him and in a most "non-analytic way" simply said: "Chaimke, bechayecha, ma ata ose kan?" The English translation would be: "Chaimke[1] come on, what are you doing here?" What I didn't think about, at that moment, is that the word "bechaye-cha", which is used in colloquial Hebrew for "come on", actually means "in your life". To my great surprise Chaim, who I had thought would just fob me off with his usual laconic but polite answer, started crying. I felt a bit uncomfortable watching this middle-aged, rather bigger-built man

---

[1] Chaimke is a common diminutive nickname for Chaim in Israel and in central Europe. It is used in informal and familial settings.

collapse and shake with sobs like a small boy, and waited silently, worried about my seemingly unprofessional intervention.

Eventually, Chaim calmed down and said that no one had called him Chaimke since his mother's death a good ten years ago. I asked him to tell me about his mother. Over several further sessions, he started to tell me his story. He was born in Germany in the early 1930s. When he was two, his father, a successful businessman worried by the rise of Nazism, managed to purchase passage for the family to Palestine. Chaim and his mother went first; the father was going to join them later after finishing arranging his affairs but was too late, and took his own life rather than face arrest and deportation to a concentration camp. Chaim's mother never spoke of his father or of her life in Germany. She forbade him to speak German and began to speak Hebrew exclusively, which he quickly mastered. Chaim's mother devoted her life to raising him to be a strong and successful boy who would fit in, and when he chose to volunteer for combat service in the army, she signed the consent form.

However, following a serious injury in one of the wars, she encouraged him to emigrate and try his luck in America. Chaim chose exile, obeying his mother's command. In the New World, he applied himself to success in business, married an American woman and had three children; he spoke no Hebrew to them and did not talk to them about his past. He continued to visit his old mother in Israel and looked after her well financially until her death. For Chaim, losing the business meant that his life had no purpose. The meaning of his life was to be successful, to survive, and to look after his mother, wife, and children. He had lived his life in a new universe—in a new language, in a new country—where trauma, separation, and loss did not exist, nor did individual attachments matter. His fetish was money and it was used to deny absence: of father, deprivation, or separation. Money had become his transitional object so that all that mattered was success: another currency for survival.

The loss of this fetish meant no psychic survival; his failure was a death sentence. Injury, loss, and pain could not be elaborated in the existing language, so following his mother's instructions, he did as she did. He assumed a new life where the past did not exist and a new safe and neutral language was acquired and a new narrative was constructed. When his business collapsed and his new world faced ruin, all he could do was, as his father did, remove himself away in the ultimate way, but not before he had made sure that his family would be safe. I came to realise that being able to use these first words in Hebrew had somehow inadvertently burst the defensive structure he had built around himself to avoid feeling the pain of his earliest traumas and losses. Repeated exiles and cut-offs became ways of not feeling, not thinking the unthinkable.

In the course of our work together feelings of loss and nostalgia began to emerge. Chaim was able to connect to his feeling of grief for the father he had lost, for his mother's losses, and for his own. He also began to value his talents, and his achievements. In the transitional space that suddenly opened between us, it was possible to replace the fetish with real objects, less fixed and frozen in time, and commence a more flexible and lively engagement. He was able to start thinking with empathy about how his children would feel if they were to lose their father, just as he did. Sometime later, Chaim agreed to meet his family with the help of the hospital social worker. Eventually he was able to hear his wife and three teenage children's expressions of love and concern for him, and chose to carry on living with his successes and failures.

In *The Man Who Never Stopped Sleeping*, Irvin/Aaron describes this process of rediscovering the link between words and their meaning, and creating a coherent whole, while in hospital, awaiting yet another operation:

> That night I slept restlessly. Pictures of the war and of the time after the war passed before me. Nothing significant bound them together. I asked myself what they were showing me and why, and I had no answer.
>
> Finally, I managed to tell myself, *Connecting the parts and giving meaning to it all are my tasks.* I was glad I had parted from the dream without depressing thoughts. (Appelfeld, 2017, p. 123)

Aaron decides to become a writer to complete his father's ambition to become one and to piece together the fragments of his experience. He wants to do it in his new language. In response to his friends who believe that one can only express oneself properly in one's mother tongue, Aaron retorts: "For years, I haven't been connected to my mother tongue. Now I expect that the Hebrew letters will link me to what's hidden inside me."

Michelle

I turn now to another clinical vignette. Michelle was a young teenage girl whom I saw in the adolescent unit, in Israel. This time I was asked to see her because I could speak English! At the age of fifteen, Michelle was a highly anxious and fearful girl. She had symptoms of OCD, with many rituals and self-harm behaviours. She was depressed and reported strong suicidal feelings. On the unit, she was bullied by the other Israeli children, and was transferred to an English-speaking unit, where she felt safer. Michelle's mother tongue was English. Her mother had arrived in the US to live with relatives after being evacuated on the Kindertransport, aged six. Her father was an Israeli war hero. The parents met in the US where they were both students and he "rescued" Michelle's mother. When Michelle was five her father moved his family back to Israel, where he took a prominent position in the business world. Michelle's mother found it difficult to adjust and became depressed and passively withdrawn.

Michelle was an only child. As a premature sickly baby she had been a great disappointment to her father. She grew up to be a serious, frail-looking young girl, and although she did very well academically and learned Hebrew very quickly, she was socially isolated, and preferred to read books and play on her own. Michelle's father was very impatient and critical of her and her mother. At times he had been physically violent and mostly regarded Michelle with contemptuous dissatisfaction. Like many traumatised children, Michelle expressed her trauma and conflicts through her body, which she divided between the left and right. Her left hand used to hit the right side of her face in a ritualised manner. She described her left side as a Nazi: evil, aggressive, sadistic, and unpredictable, out of control. Her right side was good, but weak and unworthy.

For Michelle, Hebrew was the language of fear, humiliation, and pain. She preferred to speak to me in English, to stay on her "right side". I noticed that I was speaking more softly with her, quietly, almost in whispers. It helped us think about her identification with her mother and how timidly she spoke English when she had first arrived in the US from her native Austria. She was able to think of her own similar experience, moving from her motherland and mother tongue, but also of feelings of loss and despair when she felt exiled from her mother too, as a result of her depression and withdrawal. However, we could not address her identification with the aggressor, the bully in her who attacked herself, until we came to the internalised Nazi figure. Paradoxically, we spoke Hebrew to find her. Our sessions became a playful exchange of words in both languages; at times tentatively offered by me, at times by Michelle. As she grew more confident, her self-harm behaviours stopped, as did her rituals. I felt great progress was made when she was able to freely make puns using both languages. For a long time we stayed in this space of liminality (on the threshold) until it felt safe to move beyond.

Vered

Vered (Rose in Hebrew) was a married woman in her forties, who came to see me from a remote seaside village in Scotland. She travelled a long way to see me because she wanted to work in Hebrew. She had already seen several psychotherapists over the years but, although her English was excellent, after living in the UK for over twenty years with her Scottish husband, she felt something was missing. She was a somewhat prickly, restless, and intelligent woman, who struggled with infertility and an ambivalence about having children. She felt stuck in this in-between state of wanting and not wanting to be a mother. Like Michelle, her traumas were mostly expressed in her body. She had aborted and miscarried her pregnancies several times.

Vered's parents survived the concentration camps as young teenagers. They met in a displaced people's camp and married quickly. Both were eager to resume their studies, which had been interrupted by the war. When Vered was born, both parents were working hard at university in a European capital and she was often left on her own for long hours in her crib, after being fed and changed. After her sister was born, she was left to care for her and upon completing their studies her parents reunited with one surviving grandmother and moved to Israel. The marriage broke down not long afterwards and both girls were looked after by their grandmother.

Starting our sessions in Hebrew, we soon realised that Vered had no clear sense of a mother tongue. Her mother hardly spoke to her in any language. She had no memory of a language of affection or tenderness as a small infant, except for her grandmother's Yiddish later on. Her parents spoke two different European languages and studied in a third. In our work together we came to realise how Vered needed to escape to the safety of the English language, away from family traumas and conflicts. Yet she became stuck in a safe but sterile and barren zone. Her passion was caught up in her rage at her mother for abandoning her, but how could she be angry with a mother who suffered so much? Vered's rejection of her mother and her motherland became a rejection of her own motherhood. Hebrew was the language that allowed her to express her rage but also her passion and sexuality. Eventually she decided to undergo IVF treatment with her husband and to start a family.

Transition and integration

And what about our protagonist Irvin/Aaron? In his last dream in the book he tells his mother: "I broke through the barrier, and I intend to return home" (Appelfeld, 2017, p. 287). His mother tries to dissuade him from taking the journey, especially as he has not yet healed and there are difficult things to see. But he tells her he has to see the sights with his own eyes. He has to see the Carpathian Mountains which he had carried with him all along. "Mother," he says, "I have to do it. What I don't understand, the trees and the cliffs and the hills will tell me. And if I don't see those marvels, the child who remained behind will show them to me" (p. 287). His mother, being as wise as all mothers, tells him it is too cold and dangerous, he can't take the trip on his own, and it is best to wait for his father to return from the camps: "For now, stay where you are living. Let the distant places come to you" (p. 288). This seems to me like the best attempt at transition and integration that one can hope for.

When describing his struggles with writing in the English language, Moris Farhi (2001) explains that he is able to write prose in English, but when it comes to poetry he has to wrestle with Turkish. Only after he is able to reassure the Turkish language of his love and devotion to it, can he rewrite his verses in his adopted language:

> A final word. To those who have not loved passionately more than one language, my condition might seem too stressful, traumatic even. Strangely enough, it isn't. Not any more, anyway.

It has become part of my life like an old wrestling injury. Now, I'm attached to it; I've even grown to love it. (p. 130)

References

Amati-Mehler, J., Argentieri, S., & Canestri, J. (Eds.) (1993). *The Babel of the Unconscious: Mother Tongue and Foreign Tongues in the Analytic Dimension*. Madison, CT: International Universities Press.

Appelfeld, A. (2017). *The Man Who Never Stopped Sleeping*. J. Green (Trans.). New York: Schocken.

Farhi, M. (2001). Writing in tongues. *Modern Poetry in Translation*, *17*: 128–130.

Ferenczi, S. (1933). Confusion of tongues between adults and the child: The language of tenderness and of passion. *Internationale Zeitschrift für Psychoanalyse*, *19*: 5–15.

Garland, C. (2017). Thinking about trauma. In: C. Garland (Ed.), *Understanding Trauma. A Psychoanalytical Approach* (pp. 9–31). London: Routledge.

Hoffman, E. (2008). *Lost in Translation: A Life in a New Language*. London: Vintage.

Laplanche, J., & Pontalis, J.-B. (1967). *Le Vocabulaire de la Psychanalyse*. Paris: Presses Universitaires de France.

Miletic, T. (2008). *European Literary Immigration into the French Language: Readings of Gary, Kristof, Kundera and Semprun*. Amsterdam: Rodopi.

Naficy, H. (1993). *The Making of Exile Cultures: Iranian Television in Los Angeles*. Minneapolis, MN: University of Minnesota Press.

Sa'edi, G. H. (1986). Sharh-e ahval. *Alefba*, *7*: 3–6.

Winnicott, D. W. (1982). Transitional objects and transitional phenomena. In: *Through Paediatrics to Psychoanalysis* (pp. 229–254). London: Hogarth.

CHAPTER TWO

Living in-between languages and cultures

Ali Zarbafi

Introduction

In this chapter I chart my experience of language and culture through my personal and clinical experience from Iran to England and back again. There are many languages and contexts in my life which I will discuss as ways in which I managed trauma from my early life. The theme I am developing is how I have experienced my identity and self as living in and in-between cultures, and how my identity is lodged in both where one is constantly interpreting the other.

In the beginning

As a child I had nightmares for many years where I am falling into inkblot paper. In the sky, a plane is moving in the opposite direction. My mother and father are on the plane and I can see them (her). My arms are outstretched as I fall into this darkness which is growing.

My mother tongue is English, but I had two English mothers: my mother and my grandmother. My father tongue is Farsi or, as some like to say, Persian. My father was however not interested in children and so there was no real emotional sense of him except distance. I found this language from the age of thirteen months when I arrived in Iran. My mother and father had left me in England at the age of six months with my English grandparents while they went to Iran. When I arrived in Iran seven months later, my mother was present but, I assume, psychologically lost (Robertson & Robertson, 1989). At this point I also lost my English grandparents. This "falling" into chaos, darkness, and abyss, where my mind is blotted out in this repeated nightmare is the space I imagine I was in when I arrived in Iran. I had fallen and was in shock emotionally for many years.

My Farsi language was one of play and cousins, aunts and uncles, as well as various cooks, drivers, and gardeners who played a significant role in my early life. This was a cultural language of groups. I picked up Farsi in this rather social way which probably mirrors the lack of closeness in my father but also my feeling of being outside. The Farsi language, as I experienced it, does not get anchored emotionally in one person but gets distributed among many. The group language is full of generalised affection, generosity, and of group identity, hospitality, and a sense that you are accepted within the norms of the group. I was able therefore to find comfort in this ample and affectionate group language. This group Farsi was therefore a net I fell into, but it had no real individual emotional depth for me. Even though Farsi is a deeply poetic language, full of nuance, I was not able to access its richness due to my experience of banishment. The trauma had created distance in me, so I was surviving and keeping busy but not relating in any depth to anybody. Rather like Peter Pan I had many adventures to keep away from my lost childhood or sadness (Kelley-Laine, 1997).

My family were aspiring middle-class Iranians. My father had spent a few years between the age of nineteen and twenty-three in England where he met my mother, and then lived in Germany. He was able to do well because of his command of English. Iran, in the late fifties, was a country very allied to the USA, the UK, and Europe under the Shah. This was a time of "modernisation" where everything which was Western was good for some aspiring city families. Living in Tehran, my parents' friends were a mixture of Iranian businessmen and German, French, English, and American couples who were working in the country. I remember the card games into the night, the alcohol and cigarettes, the parties, and the American cars as well as AFTV which was an American TV channel. However, most of my time was spent in the extended Iranian family, which was very large, with eleven uncles and aunts and many more cousins of various ages. Such was the power of the West in Iran that I remember clearly the day President Kennedy was assassinated in November of 1963. I felt something awful had happened in the world and I was only seven.

In Iran I liked my primary school which was a place full of games and play. Even so, I remember being picked up by the ears by a particularly sadistic male teacher in the playground. I idealised the feminine both then and later in my life, which I later understood to be a way in which I managed to keep something sacred or good alive in myself—the lost mother or potential relational self. This good place was always "over there", in a designated woman and not accessible. This feminine was also a place of feeling and desire which felt too invested with loss and terror. This changed in my late twenties when this feminine figure could no longer maintain her function for me psychically, which is when I started therapy. In Iran I found secondary school, which was all boys, a brutal and dark place and failed most of my exams.

Farsi was not, as I discovered, a language in which I could learn, as I struggled to understand and struggled at school. I was fine at maths and very good at English, but not Farsi in which most subjects were taught. I remember walking around the garden in Tehran trying to learn my subjects by rote rather than understanding them. This was generally the main form of learning for most students in a very patriarchal culture, where you were supposed to achieve and get the highest marks, rather than *understand*. Added to this cultural approach to learning, for me it was a language into which I used to escape into groups and be naughty. Its meaning was limited and possibly instrumental: a means to an end, devoid of any emotional depth. Real learning is based on curiosity which involves a secure sense of self.

When I came to England at the age of thirteen for educational reasons, or so I was told, my standard of English was poor, and I had to start a year below my year in order to catch up. However, I did well at school as I felt that I could *understand* more, and I was particularly good at making sense of the stories in the Bible and the New Testament. The Bible is full of stories of "falling" and realisations. It helped me get close, intellectually at least, and in story form, to many feelings which I had not been conscious of until I returned to England.

In England, Farsi was in the background. I spoke English with a strong accent and some boys at school mimicked my accent, and as my family name was strange, Zarbafi, I was called "Bathtub" for a while or AZ later. Although relieved to be in England as it felt emotionally easier, I was culturally at odds with Englishness which I had not experienced in any group sense except through my mother. I did not know many of the social cues one would normally know, felt slightly in my head most of the time, was good and helpful and found being a teenager in this new landscape rather alien. The activity that helped me was sport which I was good at, and this covered my social unease and made me feel part of something. In Iran sport is a very important part of social life both in families and schools. It served me as an international language and a form of communication.

I carried on at school doing fairly well at my subjects with my now limited English and got adequate grades which just about got me into university. One of my O Levels was in Persian language which I passed with a low grade. I was seen as studious, but I was not particularly bright. I was just about managing as below the surface I was always anxious and not really able to relax enough. Although I was able to understand more in English my anxiety and an internal tenseness in the mother tongue and socially in England kept me away from being fully involved in anything. Many years later I recognised this aspect of myself in the film *AI* (*Artificial Intelligence*, Steven Spielberg, 2001), in which an inventor who has lost his son creates a copy (replacement) in the form of a robot. The robot boy is adopted by a mother who activates his sense of belonging to her, only to lose her. Not understanding what has happened, the robot boy searches for his lost mother for thousands of years in an attempt to become human, which he does for a day at the end of the film. The search for meaning in this film was to go from feeling artificial to feeling real and finding real intelligence which was something I struggled with.

I carried on this search for meaning (as hinted at in the film) through reading. When I went to university I carried on learning and being educated into my mother tongue by reading and enjoying English novels as well as French and Russian literature and finally settled at university on a subject which had meaning for me—international relations! I had been doing international relations unconsciously possibly since the age of one but had not realised it. I was educated in opera, literature, and music mainly through my friends who had a variety of tastes from Puccini to Supertramp. Many of my friends were studying English so I became very familiar with novels.

I returned to Iran in 1980 just after the revolution with an idea that I may stay as I had completed my education. By this stage, however, Iran was moving fast in an authoritarian direction. These were harrowing and exciting times in Iran and I found myself in some tricky situations involving gunfire and riots. I was also quite political due to my readings and learning at university. I was now an outsider there, quite obviously, with my accented Farsi. The thing I enjoyed most was spending time with groups and families as I had always done, but another form of angry authoritarian patriarchy was now looming in the form of religious fundamentalism. I had planned curiously to work for a proposed English weekly newspaper in Tehran which was shelved due to the new Islamic and Arab vigour in the government. After five months I escaped by the skin of my teeth to Vienna in Austria on a visa, waiting to see if I could get back to England. I had an Iranian passport. Eventually after a few weeks of waiting, through my mother's endeavours, I was allowed into England on a student visa and ended up doing further postgraduate studies.

Betwixt and between

I was now lost as I had no real plan. My postgraduate studies which were mainly to do with the Middle East, Iran, and the West went on for years on a part-time basis, but I was limping along and working part-time. This academic language was one which I escaped into and I became part of a like-minded community of thinkers, as well as continuing to improve my literacy levels. The most important experience I had during this time was working at a school in Wandsworth for children who were termed "maladjusted". These were angry and violent children and I was responsible for one such boy, Daniel, who was seven and a handful. I picked him up from home, took him to school, and worked in a class of four or five children who were between seven and nine years old and who had very little concentration and were constantly challenging. I used to take Daniel home after school to meet his grim parents. When I went home at the end of the day I felt totally drained, but I had not realised that these emotionally impoverished children, whom I liked, carried a part of me, the underbelly of the doctoral student thinker. The children could not string a sentence together in written form and their language was full of violent expletives. Lunchtime at school was a harrowing experience as much of the food ended up on the floor as a symptom of how difficult it was to take anything in, rather like my inability to really take in Farsi. The school psychotherapist, I remember, had to be rescued a couple of times after being set upon by her child patient.

I later worked for an Iranian community centre in London which I enjoyed, and it felt like I was back in Iran. Most Iranians here saw me as the English bureaucrat even though I spoke the Farsi language incompletely, which gave them the edge. The point of this centre was to help Iranian exiles to learn the language and help with welfare and rights as well as organising cultural events. So now I was the English Iranian helping Iranians, but everything was about loss and compensation. Something I knew about. Later I worked for a training organisation helping young impoverished adults to learn literacy and numeracy skills or set up businesses. I was always the manager as I had the outer confidence, even though internally I was struggling and keeping my distance. I was working on the fringes rather than going for anything mainstream. I was doing something I knew internally, helping people who felt banished or outside. This was unconscious, identifying with what I was doing but not seeing my part in it. I was still waiting for something to start my adult life. This was an in-between existence as if in a waiting room somewhere waiting for my train.

Getting on the train

Eventually, after a relationship ended with an English woman, I started psychotherapy and years later decided to train. I married a non-English woman, an outsider like myself, but not Iranian or English. We were an in-between couple. I had not realised it but everything I was doing in terms of my work and marriage and now my profession was moving away from what I was expected to do as an Iranian eldest son.

I decided to train as a psychotherapist in my thirties as it seemed and felt authentic. Psychotherapy felt like the language of the thoughtful mother who could describe feelings without punishing you or frightening you. It was very comforting and meaningful. I was no longer waiting but maybe on my way, even though it may be a very bumpy ride; at least I was in the company of people who may understand what is going on.

My psychotherapy training like another language had many languages in it as the first year was mainly humanistic, whereas the last three years were analytic looking at all the analytic schools. We also had group therapy for three years with a Hungarian analyst which I found very useful. During my training I was working with an organisation called Arts for Health which was about putting arts and light into bleak NHS hospitals. This creative project possibly mirrored how I now felt in myself. After my training I started working at a refugee centre and the NHS as well as having a small private practice in my little house with two young children. These were difficult times, there was so much going on emotionally, as there generally is when you train and become a psychotherapist.

Cultural landscapes

Despite my yearning for my mother tongue, Iranian culture always felt present and part of my identity, which is not surprising given that I had spent twelve years in Iran and saw my Iranian family in England regularly as most of my family had now scattered across Europe and America. I had also returned to Iran on holidays and escaped in 1980 after the revolution. I later worked with Iranian refugees in London, so Iran was always present as a cultural landscape. I did not return for twenty years, mainly due to the Iran–Iraq war and my eligibility for conscription. I returned in the year 2000 and have visited regularly since. I remember the relief I felt on my first trip back in 2000. The relief was in that familiar smell, air, noise, bustle, and sounds and the ease with which people speak to you. My Farsi by this stage was very out of practice but I was comfortable being semi-literate as this seemed to be something I was always struggling with in both languages in various ways. This semi-literate experience is an ongoing one as in English I am often unaware of an allusion taken for granted by the people I am with and so I ask.

I am still asking in both cultures and presumably I always will be. So, in-betweenness is a fertile place but one is somehow always in the dark.

Cultures, as most anthropologists (Hawkes, 1972) observe, are how a people represent their experiences of nature through symbols and metaphors. This historic, artistic, and intellectual material enables them to understand and lead their lives interpersonally and in the context of a group who share an identity. This complete definition misses out the emotional location of such a representation, which starts for the child with the mother and family as representatives of cultural identity. When I am in Iran, I know it is Iran because of Persian carpets, handicraft, metal work, more taxis than private cars, a huge range of food, poetry, smells, the four seasons, and sounds and easy conversations. It is also a very vibrant and extrovert social space, not only in families but in any social grouping, with street vendors shouting their wares, donkeys, carts, three-wheeled little vans on the streets, and towering snow-capped mountains hanging over the city—Tehran. When I am in England, I am aware of the generally grey weather, the pubs, football, the heavy food, freedom and understanding, of being an individual, and a high level of privacy, as well as racism and class. Life is more inside than outside.

This is partly my impression which is that Iran feels more an outside experience and England a more inside experience but there is also another side to this to do with how these cultures "are" as group experiences. I know when I am in Iran because of the way people talk to each other, which is deferential depending on age and title. The word *thou* is formal and used for elders and strangers and the word *you* is informal and used for more intimate relations or siblings and friends. The idea here is that old age and elders or ones with status are important and manners are very important. Strangers are welcomed and treated in a formal way, whereas informality is intimacy. This subtle hierarchy of signs in the background which determine this type of behaviour is based on honour. Iran is an honour culture very much rooted in the identity of the family name and avoidance of shame. The group space is much more important than the individual who is there to promote the identity of the family by being successful and dutiful. One rarely uses the word "I" in Iran where everything has a group reference and many people use the plural to refer to themselves or others as groups. The notion of the master (*agha*) dominates and it is generally male and "*khanoum*" is respect for the elder woman.

You would always stand when an elder or guest walks into the room and this is not only to respect the other but to honour yourself and your family/community. Poetry is another and more ancient form of social discourse and is used as a kind of cultural profundity and beauty, and your ability to know and recite poetry gives you status and sage-like qualities in the group or the community. The individual who can cite a poetic stanza in a group conversation generally silences the group, who will show awe and respect for the speaker before moving on. This is a symbol of belonging and national pride.

Farsi sentences also end with a verb thereby making the language more dynamic in that the action arrives at the end. In Farsi my voice is louder as one has to speak when many other people are speaking generally, like making oneself heard in a group. In English by contrast my voice is much quieter as though I am not sure how to be heard in this language.

In Iran education is very important, and commands respect, especially technical qualifications such as doctor, engineer, architect, university lecturer, accountant. Lack of education diminishes your status immediately. Money is also very important as a form of status and generally trumps all other forms of social hierarchy when accompanied by a professional standing or title. In the provinces, family names are important, carrying history and patronage, as are titles which are religious or political or military. There is very little modesty around success or wealth, and these symbols including the professional status give one power and standing in this culture. These cultural ambitions and practices are all to support the honour of the family and group.

Lévi-Strauss (2004) discusses for example the importance of the familiar and the strange in culture and how cultures may interpret the same thing differently. What can and cannot be eaten takes on symbolic significance to do with belonging and home. The same applies to ideas of what is high or low, up or down, and quick and slow which vary between cultures but are given values which represent truth or nature.

On translation between cultures—John Wayne

I have noticed that many people who are bilingual or multilingual have an in-between sense of humour which is based on the quaint differences between the languages and cultures they speak. Humour is complex as it involves play, creating depth and lightness, keeping a safe distance and managing some form of anxiety creatively or aggressively as well as maintaining some authority and perspective in a group or relationship.

Thinking of humour, I have a childhood memory of watching American cowboy movies in Iran. This memory is about cultural translation or how something gets both interpreted and lost in translation. We used to watch many movies at cinemas when I was young. I remember watching lots of Westerns and they were all dubbed very well (although as a child I did not realise this consciously) so all the characters spoke Farsi.

John Wayne movies or, as our cook called him, "jon bonne", were often shown. Our cook was a simple warm-hearted woman from the countryside who had picked up this phrase as it was a familiar Iranian French import. I always remember John Wayne talking in this very downtown tough-guy Farsi which used to be interspersed with Farsi sayings. More importantly, when he turned away from the camera, "jon bonne" would start singing an Iranian folk song.

I grew up thinking that this guy was a colourful Iranian hero. The hats escaped me, but the desert landscape seemed familiar. I remember coming to England and discovering that John Wayne was dubbed in English and was very disappointed that the English had no idea how to dub this colourful Iranian guy and did not know what they were missing. He didn't even sing!

This Western cultural import into Iran—the Western, excuse the pun—was retranslated and made into something very different from anything an American could imagine in their landscape. This is also about cultural translation or how the East, playfully as it happens in this case, translates the West rather than the other way around. This bringing the West down to earth is in stark contrast to how the West traditionally interpreted the East as uncivilised and of a lower order (Said, 1978).

My own experience of therapy

Curiously, despite English being my mother tongue, my first psychotherapist was German, and spoke English with a German accent. I was born in Germany. My German psychotherapist was thoughtful and kind and showed great empathy, which is what I needed at the time to begin to understand myself. My long-term supervisors in the 1990s were a Hungarian analyst and a Chilean analyst—both had accents. One was middle school and the other Kleinian. Both were quite political due to their conflictual cultural histories in Hungary and Chile. I found all my supervisors inspiring in different ways. When I was looking for my second analyst, I asked my Hungarian supervisor who suggested I go to see an Italian analyst and at this point I wondered if it may be an idea to see an English analyst, if there was such a thing. In the end I did see an English analyst and he was Jungian and also, I learnt later, Irish, without an accent. My English analyst was recommended by my second long-term supervisor who is Austrian and Jungian.

My experience with my English analyst was profound and I mined many dreams for many years in our sessions, revisiting the trauma of my early life, understanding why I knew about loss and the refugee experience as a child, as well as opening up my thinking and empathy more creatively than before. Many of my dreams seemed to carry images of both Iran and England in them. The dreams were showing this sense of dual identity as well as how they were inextricably laced together. The inkblot paper or darkness that existed in my childhood nightmares had turned into a dense pattern of intertwined meanings and possibilities and I have spent years writing out these dreams with ink.

A key dream was the following.

> I am away from my house (home) and get a phone call from my wife that our daughter, my first child who is still seven or eight has died. I feel terrible and come back in a daze and enter the house but notice that there are many decorators now coming in and out and our home is being changed without my permission. I am annoyed that this is going on at such a time, but it is just happening. Instead of the wooden floors there are now thick carpets and our modern furniture has been replaced by thick big furniture reminiscent of my grandparents. There is an old-fashioned fireplace now in the room rather than a radiator. The kitchen now has two entrances where there was only one before. One entrance is a square door and the other door has a crescent shape at the top. I go up into the bedroom and there are now instead of photos three symbols on our walls which were not there before,

of a knight, a queen, and a prince framed like one may see in a church ... I wake up very upset, unable to go back to sleep again.

This dream was a key moment in my life as, first, I was able to dream it, and second, it was clear that the dream, with deep feelings, was showing me how I coped with the loss of the feminine feeling part of myself through an elaborate more cushioned psychological defence. I am protected from the real with carpets and old sofas, grandparents, and more options for feeding, including the Islamic door as well as idealised Christian symbols instead of photos. I have been transported psychically away from what has happened to a symbolic space where I imagine I lived for many years before therapy finally enabled me to understand the trauma. This symbolic place housed me until I could face the affect and mourn the loss which is what this dream faced me with. It is also a very good demonstration of how dreams can work to show us what is unconscious and what mechanisms can be used to protect the self.

This dream of loss and the imaginative defence against it merely confirmed the importance of dreams for me, from the nightmares of youth to the many dreams I brought to my analyst. So social dreaming was not a big step for me as I felt the power of this unconscious ability which we have both individually and socially, reflecting my own experience of how the group and the individual are inextricably linked. In the next few years after the year 2000, as well as returning to Iran frequently, I became intensely involved in social dreaming with both Gordon Lawrence and John Clare which led to an article and a book with John. At the same time, I wrote a training module charting the refugee journey with a Kurdish Iranian colleague, Arsalan Ghalieh. We ran these workshops for organisations around the country that worked with refugees to give them a better understanding of the experience by taking them through it using group work. Meanwhile I was also involved in the Multi-lingual Psychotherapy Centre, who were a group of exiles or outsiders living in London. We were all psychotherapists or analysts. A member once called this an "exilic" space which sounded rather like perfume to me or the word exotic.

Giving the refugee experience a shape, respecting difference in the multilingual experience, and allowing dreams to be seen as both social and personal have given me a language in which I can express myself. These endeavours cross cultures. This is where I locate my language and feeling of authority. This is where I speak from and feel most comfortable. All three have pain and potential in them.

The third language

I have worked with many patients, in English or with an interpreter, whose first language is not English. There is what I would call a third language which emerges in therapy, a form of psychic patois, in which the therapist and patient slowly learn each other's languages and cultures, and this is helped by the other non-verbal communications present in the room. This I would think of as the transitional space as elaborated by Winnicott (1953), which is a third area of experience between mother and child where illusion and reality dance and play, where the child's mind creates and elaborates and paradox exists, without being questioned. This is the location of cultural and psychological creativity necessary in any therapeutic encounter for an internal sense of authorship and agency.

The patient basically wants to be understood and have a sense that the therapist is interested in knowing him or her. This is of course a metaphor for the relationship between inside and outside where identity and self are located. If the patient feels like an outsider, the need to be known is even greater. Both are working hard, and language is not necessarily the main way in which communication is happening.

Many languages have different ways of describing intimacy and the analyst/therapist needs to be aware that for many non-European cultures the description of intimacy is always obtuse and is more understood and understated than spoken. So, it becomes a case of what "can" be spoken both culturally and emotionally. The second language can help in these cases but there may not be an equivalent emotional language in the mother tongue. A Chinese patient of mine described her Cantonese mother tongue as "rubbish", as it was for her only a social or action language with no intimacy. In the work, she experienced me as careful, but it transpired that this was a projection of the danger she felt in expressing feelings which she felt I would not be able to contain, like the Cantonese mother.

Conclusion

The relationship between the individual and the group and the cultural context of meaning is one of my main themes in this chapter and in my experience. Trauma is a central theme for me as it has determined how I have gone from shock to survival to a slow rediscovery and thawing of my ability to think, feel, and reflect in both languages. I would say that transforming affect into feelings and then thinking has been the main journey I have been on in these different languages and cultures which have allowed me different spaces. The cultural weight and significance of feelings will vary among different cultures which is why the "other" is always strange, interesting, and challenging. This is about the complex relationship that exists between the group and the individual and which collective ideas and practices dominate individual spaces and allow for different psychic possibilities and limits.

Iranian culture and language provided me with a large group space, which was containing and affectionate, where I could play and forget my individual loss. English culture and language faced me with an early meaningful resonance in which I had to face my individual struggles and the need for connection, meaning, and understanding. This was a lost but potential interior space. I now feel more comfortable in both languages and cultures, which now complement each other and are more integrated.

A Japanese colleague of mine, who had been educated in English and French from the age of seven, told me that her Japanese language always "whispered" to her in the background. I often think of language rather like symbols which flower after a long seasonal process involving nature and culture and family in all its density.

I am clear that within my English and Iranian languages and cultures, I have learnt to speak many other languages in my life, from international relations to cultural anthropology, and politics to psychotherapy, the refugee experience and social dreaming. They have all helped me to try to make sense of that blotting paper. In psychotherapy I went from Laing to Freud to Winnicott and finally ended up with Jung mainly because of dreams and Jung's interest in the collective. However, I find all these psychotherapy languages interesting and valuable in their own right. There is no truth, only felt stories which can be remembered and reflected upon and where we find our sense of identity and meaning. This was always clear in our multilingual lectures as well as the discussions we had as multilingual colleagues where something was always hidden and then found and then lost again. Ultimately, despite everything, I find myself always going back to the beginning with the experience and language of child development which in its pure intensity and aliveness, like the sail on the boat, propels us into the great sea of life.

References

Hawkes, T. (1972). *Metaphor.* Bristol, UK: Methuen.

Kelley-Laine, K. (1997). *Peter Pan: The Story of Lost Childhood.* Shaftesbury, UK: Element.

Lévi-Strauss, C. (2004). *The Savage Mind.* Oxford: Oxford University Press.

Robertson, J., & Robertson, J. (1989). *Separation and the Very Young.* London: Free Association.

Said, E. W. (1978). *Orientalism.* London: Routledge & Kegan Paul.

Winnicott, D. W. (1953). Transitional objects and transitional phenomena—a study of the first not-me possession. *International Journal of Psychoanalysis, 34*(2): 89–97.

CHAPTER THREE

Childhood, spoken and written selves

Natsu Hattori

Introduction

> I have crossed an ocean
> I have lost my tongue
> from the root of the old one
> a new one has sprung
>
> "Epilogue" by Grace Nichols (2010)

I begin with voyages, with loss, pain, growth, and new beginnings, as Grace Nichols says. The blend of received ideas and personal experience here recalls Lévi-Strauss's concept of "the raw and the cooked" (1969) as basic categories of human thought. This made me think of "soup", more specifically, the miso soup that traditionally Japanese people eat at breakfast. Like most soups, it has a bit of everything: miso soup is made from a base of fermented soya bean paste and fish stock: both these ingredients require prior and lengthy preparation, even though these days they come ready-made for the kitchen. Into this mix, it's usual to drop in different uncooked ingredients: fresh-cut vegetables, spring onion, as well as tofu and so on.

I speak in this chapter of my relationship with my mother tongue. My memories and reflections are the tofu and spring onions I've chopped and dropped into a soup that has been bubbling for generations. The rich base of stock, however, is the work of linguists, anthropologists, psychologists, and novelists, all of whom have studied these questions of language, identity, migration, and culture.

My own history of language and migration

I was born in the seaside town of Tsu, in Mie Prefecture, near the invisible borderline between Western and Eastern Japan. My parents came from Western Japan: my mother from a sprawling village on the delta formed by the confluence of two great rivers, the Kiso and Nagara, flowing into the Pacific Ocean. My father came from a small but historically significant town in the mountains which was on the traditional route between Kyoto and Edo (now Tokyo), the rival seats of the imperial and shogunate governments of the country before the nineteenth century.

I have spent nearly all my life in the West, thinking, speaking, acting as a Westerner; first in Canada where I moved with my family at the age of five. I came to England in my early twenties, and also spent some time in Mexico and Brazil as an adult.

My whole life has been in part a turning away from my roots, immersing myself in British and European and American (as in both North and South American) languages, cultures, and habits. I read Western literature as a child; I trained in Western theatre as a teenager; learned French, Latin, and German in school; studied European literature and history at university and, worked as a postdoctoral researcher and lecturer in English renaissance drama and history in Oxford, London, and York.

I now work as a Gestalt psychotherapist in London, practising a modality founded in central European psychology and philosophy, and developed in the 1950s by German refugees to the US. It now has centres around the world, including in Japan where the first international meeting took place in 2011. The YouTube video of that meeting shows a sometimes comical mix of West and East, with a "therapy circle" formed on tatami mats, a performance by taiko drummers, and many different pronunciations of "Gestalt".

The Gestalt therapy principles (Perls, Hefferline, & Goodman, 1951) that permeate my thinking are:

1) Field theory, adapted from physics by German social psychologists to describe the interconnected and embedded nature of persons and their environment, and the importance of not taking any phenomenon or psychological event in isolation, but as part of a whole
2) The dialogic relationship; and the intersubjective connection between self and other, the co-created nature of experience.

Why, now, do I have an urge to look at my roots? At my time of life, like the grey that keeps seeping up in my hair through the dye, my roots seem to need attention.

And a scene from Paulo Sorrentino's 2013 film *La Grande Bellezza* comes to mind; when a revered and elderly nun of ascetic habits speaks with the man-about-town protagonist, Gep Gambardella:

> *Suor Maria: E sa, perche io mangio solo radici?*
> *Gep: No. No, perche?*
> *Suor Maria: Perche le radici sono importanti.*

> [Sister Maria: And do you know why I eat only roots?
> Gep: No. No, why?
> Sister Maria: Because roots are important.]

Migration and identity

My awareness for many years of the long-standing effects on me of my childhood migration was clouded by my own creative adjustment as a child: I quietly accepted the necessity of "getting on and getting along", finding my place in a new environment; and discovering ways of belonging and feeling more or less "at home". From the protection and seclusion of family life in Japan, I found myself transported into a different country, an unfamiliar social environment full of adults and children none of whom knew me or knew the language I spoke. To survive, I needed to master new skills: a new language, new gestures and forms of embodiment; as well as to familiarise myself with new foods, places, and cultural practices. In making these adjustments, the use of my mother tongue was largely displaced by my adoptive language, as I forsook subtle bodily and non-verbal forms of communication which were appropriate in my family and cultural background but led to mis-understandings in the society to which I'd been transplanted. The plasticity of childhood, and the overriding need to "fit in" and be accepted, meant that for me, many of these adaptations occurred within the first year after arriving in Canada. And there were other losses: the absence of our extended family and its networks of support; our relative lack of embeddedness in cultural and social networks, and the shared histories of the wider community. My later migrations as an adult repeated many of these challenges, although my adjustments regarding embodiment, language, and culture were never as comprehensive or deep-seated as the first time.

Many studies of migration and psychotherapy tend to focus on the aspects of loss, trauma, and annihilation of the self that take place in a person whose very existence *as* himself is denied by others, or defined in ways which are alienating or destructive to the self (Eleftheriadou, 2010; Fanon, 2001). With the emphasis on adaptation and the price this carries, the overriding impression presented by these studies is of the negative and destructive impact of colonisation and displacement, and the pervasive influence of racism and cultural hegemony on the "minority" subject.

Migration involves far-reaching change: geographic, cultural, and linguistic. It also can precipitate a crisis of identity for the migrant. Previously held certainties may be threatened or compromised: beliefs regarding who she is, her physical as well as social location, her role in family structures, as well as familiar customs and forms of expression both bodily and verbal. One becomes estranged from oneself. The experience can be profoundly destabilising and alienating; it can feel as if the very ground of experience has shifted in unfathomable ways, removing all safety and security. The migrant may not recognise herself in the unfamiliar ways people now relate to her and in how she must relate to them; she may find herself, as the Polish Canadian writer Eva Hoffman (1998) writes, "becoming a strange kind of creature I never meant to turn into" (p. 79).

And at the same time, migration can represent the opportunity to reshape, transform, and reinvent the self; and to undo the fixity of mono-cultural beliefs and structures in favour of a more flexible way of being. Migration can provide an alternative to old family and social systems which can be oppressive or limiting: sometimes the change of country and identity is "*the making*" of immigrants. My own parents when young, felt stifled by the traditions and homogeneity of Japanese culture, where society was rigidly based on deference to authority, and family systems of interdependency could lead to intrusive scrutiny and a lack of respect for individual wishes. Their gain from migrating to a more individualistic and less hierarchical society was a new sense of freedom and validation of their personal choices. While they remained largely "strangers" in their adopted country, the openness and tolerance of a multicultural society allowed them a different sense of "belonging".

Early life: divided by dialect, language, and culture

My earliest aural memories are of singing folk songs taught to me by my maternal grandmother. Descended from a samurai clan, she was taught as a young girl to throw *shuriken*, small daggers at opponents' heads. Her sisters were each taught a different martial art: archery, sword-fighting, and so on. Her songs were all about battles, and my favourite one was a twenty-stanza-long epic, of which sadly I now only recollect the first line: "*Daikoku san to yu hito wa*" ("Daikoku-san was a person like this …", a Japanese version of "Telling of arms and the man"); it was a tale of military exploits and the glories and hardships of war.

These songs, like all my early verbal memories, were taught to me in the Kansai dialect, or the particular form of it spoken by my grandmother who was raised on ancestral lands in the mountain district of Hirano, east of Kyoto and inland from Nagoya. My family and my early life were divided by dialect: both my grandmothers and my father were from Western Japan where they speak the Kansai dialect used in Kyoto and Osaka; my mother and maternal grandfather, both educated in Tokyo, spoke in the "standard" Kanto dialect, which is what Westerners learn when they are taught Japanese.

The sound, intonation, and vocabulary of the two dialects are not the only differences: there are strong differences in food preferences, sense of humour, style of dress, and "character" types associated with the West and the East of Japan. For a Westerner like my father, people from Tokyo were "strait-laced, conventional, and hypocritical"; to Tokyo denizens like colleagues and friends I met later in life, people from Kyoto were "arrogant and incompetent", and their accent was inherently comical. A lot of stand-up comics in the *rakugo* style were Kansai speakers.

As Gecele puts it,

> Language has the power to include and exclude, to define experiences, abstractions and types of relationship … Every child traces a path starting with his or her native language … In his evolution, the child acquires a relational competence that allows him or her to stay at the contact boundary, and to feel the void, the absence … a continuous and arduous process of translation, an attempt to express, reach others and shape the world. (Francesetti et al., 2013, pp. 216–217)
>
> What is the experience of a child who lives in a country where the spoken language is not that of his parents? A child whose parents often do not "know" the names of things? A child learning a new language, or more than one language at the same time, can structure a world, many worlds, more or less complete, friendly or threatening. Different ways of telling the same story may interweave or take parallel courses. (Francesetti et al., 2013, p. 217)

When I was three, my family and I spent two years in the US when my father took up a research position. While I absorbed the English language through the television, and learned simple words and the alphabet, linguistically I remained Japanese, immured in my family, and playing mostly with the children of Japanese families my parents met in the university town where they lived. The Kanto dialect began to dominate over the Kansai dialect in my speech and thinking, as I spent more time with my mother and my Tokyo-born playmates.

My mother and I returned to Japan for six months when I was five: my paternal grandfather was dying of stomach cancer. Once again, I was in the realm of my grandmother, and her language and stories; of fearsome mountain hags, *Yamam-ba*, who lured travellers to their forest homes, and killed and ate them; of shape-shifting animal spirits and ghouls, often also female, who revealed their true nature on their wedding nights to their unlucky spouses. Worst of all, the soft-spoken stranger you encounter in the dark forests, whom at first you greet with relief as a companion on the lonely journey, and who walks step by step alongside you, until in a remote clearing, the stranger turns towards you and you see that *he has no face ...*

My grandmother told me these tales as we huddled by the under-table heater on cold winter mornings, while my mother was busy tending to my grandfather upstairs.

It was in this waiting period, while spending time alone in my grandparents' house, that I was given an exercise book with the Japanese alphabet and began to teach myself to read and write in *hiragana* and *katakana*. This was my earliest writing self. The first story which I wrote was in Japanese. Now, many decades later, I have forgotten what I knew, and cannot write as well in Japanese as I could then. This is a source of great sadness and shame to me; it is not easy for me to return after all these years to my first exploratory ventures in writing in my mother tongue. Which is why it has probably taken me this long to address these questions for myself.

The end of this time was marked by my grandfather's death, after which my mother and I rejoined my father, this time in Canada, which became my parents' permanent home. This was my parents' moment of true expatriation, when they elected to leave their country of origin for good and make their way in a foreign land. It was also when our family formed as a nuclear unit, detached from our extended family, whom we saw only once every four or five years subsequently.

It was the moment also when I entered an alien world, going to school on the west coast of Canada. At that point in time, I could not speak or understand any English at all. I entered a kindergarten reception class halfway through the year. I recall, as if through a mist, the classroom sounds swirling around me, words and sentences falling past my ears like autumn leaves, my eyes catching gestures, beginning to understand them, but unable to respond. My teacher rang my mother to inform her that in her opinion, I was "hard of hearing". My musician mother who had taught me singing and piano since the age of three was puzzled. She asked why the teacher thought so. "Well, she doesn't answer when she's spoken to." My mother replied cryptically, and accurately: "I think you will find that her hearing will improve with time."

My teacher's perception of my "deafness" in a sense contained an element of truth because without an ability to understand what was spoken, I was unable to attune my hearing to my environment. This alienation is captured by the Australian Gestalt therapist Greta Leung (2010), who describes how, living in Hong Kong in a "congested, densely populated Chinese community where the English language was not spoken" she experienced herself "as if deaf and dumb" (p. 21). Eva Hoffman describes her bodily experience as a teenager transplanted from Poland to Canada:

> My gestures show that I'm here provisionally ... that I don't rightfully belong. My shoulders stoop, I nod frantically to indicate my agreement with others, I smile sweetly at people to show I mean well, and my chest recedes inward so that I don't take up too much space ..., mannerisms of a marginal, off-centered person who wants both to be taken in and to fend off the threatening others. (1998, p. 110)

Being faced with not being able to speak or communicate in a new culture can be a deeply humbling experience. My memory of learning to speak in English was not of a gradual acquisition, but of a sudden "switching on" of a capacity: in keeping with the "deafness" metaphor, it was as if I "tuned in" on a radio dial, and from that moment I could understand everything that was said around me: a murmuring buzz was transformed to words, sentences; the dead leaves became hovering creatures I could capture and myself breathe life into. I went from deafness and immobility in language to hearing, speaking, walking, running, jumping in my second language.

> Foreigners frequently master the grammar of a language better than its native speakers, the better, perhaps, to hide their difference, their diffidence, which also explains why they are so tactful, almost ceremonial, when it comes to the language they adopt.... How do you indeed, can you ever rebuild a home? What kinds of shifts must take place for a person to acquire, let alone accept, a new identity, a new language? (Aciman, 1994, pp. 12–14)

In making these shifts, I also lost a great deal: the original relational competence developed in my mother tongue(s), the opportunity to use this in the wider world, and the non-verbal communication learned in the embodied culture of my origins. In my seemingly fluid adaptation to a new environment, my seamless adoption of the habits and mannerisms of people around me, how much was I continuing to miss, in unspoken rules, body language, social cues, and customs too subtle and too culturally embedded and "given" to be easily accessible or comprehensible to me as a child and while growing up? And to what extent is my position as "an outsider" still with me after all these years?

The South African/Dutch artist Marlene Dumas describes this state of mind in her poem:

"Not From Here" (1994)

… I am always "not from here",
even though I try to know,
or understand "what's going on" and
what the rules are and how they
keep on changing and what that means.
When looking at images I'm not lost,
but I'm uneasy.

(Van den Berg & Dumas, 1998, pp. 82–84)

"A French saint once said that it is as dangerous for a writer to try a new language as it is for a believer to try a new religion: he can lose his soul" (Caetano Veloso album cover, 1971).

Growing up and away: from West to East (or East to West)

There is a particular creative quality associated with being on the boundary of the known and not known. A liminal position holds fear and uncertainty, but at the same time it is ripe with potential: with hope, possibilities, and excitement. The "boundary situation" of migration brings upheaval, change, and disturbance of previously held beliefs about oneself and others. Like other major life events or crises, it can represent

danger as well as opportunity (Yalom, 1980, p. 35). Gestalt therapy provides a theoretical underpinning for the existential self-reinvention of
the migrant, who travels not only temporally from past to future, from
the familiar to the unknown, but performs this transit in space: from a
known place to one unfamiliar and strange.

In the experience of migration there is a tension between two polari-
ties: the individual desire for mobility, autonomy, and self-expression,
and the animal/social need for rootedness, belonging, and relation. This
is a polarity present in all humans (Spagnuolo Lobb & Amendt-Lyon,
2003, p. 121); yet in the case of migration it can be amplified by divisions
of geography, culture, language, and history between the migrant and
her new community. This leads to the creation of multiple identities,
multiple selves (Moodley & Palmer, 2006), which can produce the alienation and depersonalisation experienced by many migrants and exiles.
Yet it can also inspire the creative assimilation and integration found
in art, literature, and psychologies produced by the migrant/expatriate
or exile.

Having to speak, and write, in different languages involves a translation of meaning, "a specific and complex mode of creative adjustment"
(Francesetti et al., 2013, p. 218). A bilingual writer/speaker engages in a
shuttling back and forth between two modes of thinking and expressing
himself. I have observed that people can feel differently, as I do, when
using their different languages and that expressing certain emotions
carries a different emotional resonance depending on the language one
is using.

> Changing the reference language changes the frame of reference
> in which the person lives and builds a sense of his or her own life.
> At a given point contents and experience pass through a junction,
> turning from an old story to a new one.... The two languages,
> the two worlds can interact in a constructive or disruptive way.
> (Francesetti et al., 2013, p. 218)

While disorienting, especially initially, with time and practice this creates
a greater flexibility, and widens one's awareness and perspective, creating
one may say a dual perspective. As the historian Chandak Sengoopta
says: "I have always found English to be the easiest language to write in

and Bengali the best language for speaking, thinking and daydreaming" (2004, p. 267). Hoffman writes: "I learn English through writing and in turn, writing gives me a written self … This language is beginning to invent another me" (1998, p. 121). In discovering her "writing self", Hoffman sees how the triangulations she learned through her experience of negotiating difference have taught her the skills, the polyvalent consciousness she uses as a historian and critic.

Similarly, I created, from "deaf and dumb" beginnings, an English/Canadian or European self; such was my relational need to develop my linguistic capacity that I began in time to "specialise" in speaking/performing/writing/thinking in words. From a childhood immersed in books, I developed a persona and social world based on speaking, hearing, writing, performing, culminating in my current work as a therapist. Moving from the metaphor of "deafness" it is as if, having lost my "legs" in one language, I proceeded to compete in athletic events in my prosthetic or self-generated replacement limbs.

Meanwhile, in my family as I grew up, we all began to live in two concurrent, overlapping modes; the English-speaking world of work, school, society, which overlaid or intersected with the Japanese world of family. Part of this involved a separation of spheres: English outdoors, Japanese indoors. My parents often literally changed their clothes on arriving home: a not uncommon Japanese custom. Or, as in my case increasingly, I wore my outdoor clothes inside the house, and spoke to my parents in English, while they replied in Japanese. This never struck me as odd until I was presented with the mystified reaction of friends who visited our house and witnessed these bilingual conversations.

Sometimes it also involved a practice known to linguists as "code switching", which is typically defined in linguistics as a mixing of languages and speech patterns in conversation (Woolford, 1983).

If for my parents the body was Japanese, and English simply a set of clothes they wore to interact with Canadians and others, and they largely shed the clothes on entering the house, for me as a child, it was more complicated: the body which was Japanese was and is still five or six years old, and all the overlaying growth was in my second language. And yet, I am physically still Japanese, racially instantly recognisable to most Japanese. So what am I, really?

And back again: refamiliarisation with origins; the return of the repressed?

For many years, what was "unfamiliar" to me was my Japanese self. In my self-creation and relational impetus to make my way in the West, I largely disowned my mother tongue, such was the void and terror (still unarticulated, half understood) left by the devalidation of my mother tongue in my school life, that I must have needed to make this adjustment to feel safe in my new environment.

Lately, however, I began to pay attention to all the ways in which my mother tongue is still my own. I mentioned the image of my five-year-old Japanese self. It's also as if my viscera, my guts are still Japanese; or as if neurologically my mother tongue is still nestled, not in my centres of reasoning and logic where most of my verbal capacity is held, but in my feeling-sense, my deepest memories, the snatches of song, repeated phrases, murmuring of voices around me which may be the earliest sounds I heard, and which return to me in dreams, in certain moments when my mind is at rest and open to reverie and the music of my first and smallest self. Curiously, despite my many years of studying French or Italian and other languages, Japanese remains the easiest language, besides English, for me to eavesdrop.

On the rare occasions when I return to Japan, I notice a similar phenomenon to my first "tuning in" to English, occurring in reverse, though less dramatically. Words and phrases and manners of speech I never consciously recall flood back to me in response to the torrent of Japanese I hear spoken all around me.

Speaking now in my mother tongue, I am halting; hesitant, ashamed. Although my "passive" knowledge, from years of listening to my parents and others, surpasses that of most non-native speakers, my "active" use of Japanese has atrophied, my original limbs mere stumps compared to my sleek prosthetic English arms and legs. I can sound Japanese on short acquaintance, in conversation about the kind of things that six year olds are interested in. But stay with me a bit longer, and my small store of speech subsides, leaving me staring, either unable to breathe, a fish out of water, or, when less anxious, simply finding myself recalling the "deaf and dumb" child who entered a different language from the other direction. As I was "lost" in a new language then, before "finding" a new version of myself in it, I am confused, disoriented, ashamed, and mournful when I return to the linguistic space of my early life, and find the houses and streets abandoned, or full of strangers I don't know.

> There are two kinds of homes: the home of our childhood and origin, which is a given, a fate, for better or for worse, and the home of our adulthood, which is achieved only through an act of possession, hard-earned, patient, imbued with time, a possession made of our choice, agency, the labour of understanding, and gradual arrival. We need to develop a model in which the force of our first legacy can be transposed or brought into dialogue with our later experiences, in which we can build new meanings as valid as the first ones. This can be done only through a deepening investigation, through familiarization. (Hoffman, 1998, pp. 60–62)

Every relationship is, in a way, a translation (Gecele, in Francesetti et al., 2013, p. 215). Hoffman uses translation as a metaphor for empathy across a cultural divide; and also for self-transformation though therapy. "A true translation," she writes, is "a shift in the innermost ways … it proceeds by the motions of understanding and sympathy, it happens by slow increments, sentence by sentence, phrase by phrase" (1998, p. 211). Therapy for Hoffman is also, "partly translation therapy, the talking cure, the second-language cure … I keep going back and forth over the rifts, not to heal them but to see that I, one person, first-person singular, have been on both sides" (pp. 271–273).

There are many examples of writers, artists, psychoanalysts, and psychotherapists who have been on "both sides": it is noteworthy how many founding practitioners of psychoanalysis, and of Gestalt therapy, were themselves migrants or exiles; and worked in a language other than their own mother tongue (Eleftheriadou, 2010). There are also contemporary writers who have similarly crossed a linguistic divide, including Kazuhiro Ishiguro, who left Japan at the age of five, settled in England, and grew up to become one of the best-known writers in Britain.

Among contemporary Japanese writers, Haruki Murakami is one not only found in translation … but one who *found himself* in translation. He wrote the opening pages of his first novel, *Hear the Wind Sing*, in English, then translated those pages into Japanese, as he said, "just to hear how they sounded" (Kelts, 2008).

Conclusion

I have now started to return and retranslate myself but this is challenging and this was highlighted to me by a Japanese patient. She came from the forest island of Shikoku and left Japan at eighteen to study in the UK. She married into an English family but is now separated. She spent many sessions "facing the demon" of her ferocious inner critic, who started out speaking Japanese but has gradually switched to English: "*hetakuso*" (clumsy, inept), "*yowamushi*" (weakling), "*baka*" (stupid), now become "waste of space", "failure", "worthless". These words haunted me as I realised that my protected journey had a shadow of guilt and shame, sitting, watching me from the Japanese culture of honour which I secretly held inside me.

References

Aciman, A. (1994). *Out of Egypt: A Memoir.* New York: Riverhead.

Eleftheriadou, Z. (2010). *Psychotherapy and Culture: Weaving Inner and Outer Worlds.* London: Karnac.

Fanon, F. (2001). *The Wretched of the Earth.* London: Penguin.

Francesetti, G., Gecele, M., Roubal, J., & Greenburgy, L. (2013). *Gestalt Therapy in Clinical Practice: From Psychopathology to Aesthetics of Contact.* Siracusa, Italy: Istituto de Gestalt.

Hoffman, E. (1998). *Lost in Translation: A Life in a New Language.* London: Vintage.

Kelts, R. (2008). *Japanamerica: How Japanese Pop Culture Has Invaded the US.* Basingstoke, UK: Palgrave Macmillan.

Leung, G. (2010). *A Gestalt Perspective on the Phenomenal World of Addiction. Gestalt Journal of Australia and New Zealand,* 6(2): 20–38.

Lévi-Strauss, C. (1969). *The Raw and the Cooked: Introduction to the Science of Mythology.* London: Penguin, 1986.

Moodley, R., & Palmer, S. (2006). *Race, Culture and Psychotherapy: Critical Perspectives in Multi-cultural Practice.* Hove, UK: Routledge.

Nichols, G. (2014). *I Have Crossed the Ocean.* Hexham, UK: Bloodaxe.

Perls, F. S., Hefferline, R., & Goodman, P. (1951). *Gestalt Therapy: Excitement and Growth in the Human Personality.* Santa Barbara, CA: Gestalt Journal Press.

Sengoopta, C. (2004). A passion for dipthongs. *History Workshop Journal, 57*: 263–270.

Spagnuolo Lobb, M., & Amendt-Lyon, N. (2003). *Creative License: The Art of Gestalt Therapy.* New York: Springer.

Van den Berg, M., & Dumas, M. (1998). *Marlene Dumas: Sweet Nothings, Notes and Texts.* Amsterdam: Uitgeverij de Balle.

Woolford, E. (1983). *Bilingual Code-Switching and Syntactic Theory. Linguistic Inquiry, 14*(3): 520–536.

Yalom, I. (1980). *Existential Psychotherapy.* New York: Basic Books.

CHAPTER FOUR

When the mother tongue is contaminated

Patricia Gorringe

Introduction

So many of the stories I hear in my multicultural and multiracial practice are painful stories of separation and loss. Because many of the clients I see are physically separated from their homelands, their stories are not merely the articulation of loss through the separation from the mother, but the result of a further double separation—from *mother*land and mother tongue. This process of exile is abrupt and harsh and is more often than not accompanied by some kind of severe trauma. While there is always grief at the loss, there is also, sometimes, a relief at being safe. There is invariably always pain.

Working in such a practice as this requires an acute awareness of "difference", and, I believe, a positive therapeutic listening. There also needs to be an understanding that there will be palimpsestic layers of suffering. I use the word "palimpsestic" because, like those ancient texts or artworks which have been inscribed and painted over leaving physical traces of an earlier form, this memory of suffering, layered with the colours of different cultural and social milieus, seems also to express itself physically. The clients' struggle to enter into and use language overwhelms them as they try to access their memories. It is common for them to access other, more physical modes of communication such as silence, physical repetition (like rocking, nodding, or scratching) to express themselves and, as therapists, we have to listen to this. Sometimes they seem to hold themselves physically to comfort or contain themselves in the face of the therapist, whom they mistrust and of whom they feel afraid.

Some of these clients feel like young children in the room and this has complex repercussions and questions for the therapy. Thus, a key issue we face in our work relates to how we manage this struggle to express the unexpressible and we ask whether there are similarities between this struggle and the original birth into language. From a practical perspective, we are also concerned with managing and working with the physicality of these clients and how we listen to their trauma.

Like my clients, the world I once knew no longer exists, for better or for worse. Although I have been physically absent from my homeland for decades, the textures, the lights, and colours of my childhood still filter through my dreams where the powerful umbilical cord of the motherland tugs at my belly. In the landscapes of my sleep, the burnt-brown rounded *kopjes* (hillocks) of the African bush throw shadows on the dense rich fields of the new world of England creating a kind of palette of shades and shapes as multicoloured daubs on acrylic. Like many exiles, I find myself almost fitting into the new world, yet being part of the old one. We live in limbo in the shadows, part of the darkness and part of the light. Because my story is also one of exile and loss, my interface with and my reactions to the inner world of my clients bears the marks of my experience.

My journey and exile

My story begins with a physical leaving, a migration from the land of my birth, Zimbabwe, in my mid-teens. This was a journey forced upon my family by war and by the loss of my own mother to a stroke, a dramatic and life-changing event. The loss of multiple mothers was significant; leaving (and losing) my motherland resulted in my leaving and losing another mother, the Ndebele woman who had loved and looked after me from birth and whom I would never see again—she would be raped and beaten to death during "Gukurahundi", a series of massacres of Ndebele civilians carried out by the Shona-dominated Zimbabwe National Army from early 1983 to late 1987. Deriving from the Shona language term which loosely translates to "the early rain which washes away the chaff before the spring rains", it is estimated that this genocide took the lives of at least 20,000 Zimbabweans.

Separation, loss, and violence dominated my early life and this was to have psychic repercussions for me as I moved geographically from Africa to Europe and to the United States in my adult life. Many of the brutal stories of my childhood are therefore part of a secret past that cannot be talked about, a past that is drenched in shame. When I finally left Africa in my mid-twenties to live in the United States, I became overwhelmed by terrible grief and a profound sense of loss, but because of my shame, I could not speak of this. I found myself wondering why America felt so strange and alien and the people so foreign, when we all spoke the same language? I fell into a very dark depression and sought help in analysis. However, when I arrived at the analyst's rooms, I found I could not speak. For months I sat in complete silence for the full fifty minutes, wringing my hands. Decades later I am able to recall with total clarity what the room looked like, where the clock was, the fireplace, the chair, and the kind face of the therapist, but the terror of speaking was too great.

Through my work with clients and my own analysis, I have come to think about my silence as a way of communicating something which cannot be expressed in language because it is forbidden and shameful and too painful to bear. John Clare (2004), amongst others, has commented on how some patients use the tongue of their adopted country in therapy to give them some psychic space, away from the burden of loss this exile brings, precisely because it facilitates their need to speak about the unspeakable. Some patients have the option to use a second language, but for some like me, this is not an option. What this has given me in my work as a therapist is insight into how traumatised exiles can use silence and physicality as a means of communicating the inexpressible, and this is what I am going to attempt to explore in this chapter.

The language of the inner world

It is not really surprising that my longing for another language to speak about my inner world resulted in my interest in psychoanalysis and it is no accident that I chose to write my university thesis on Julia Kristeva, a post-Lacanian thinker. To summarise Lacan's ideas is an impossible task, but for the sake of clarity let me set out some basic tenets. Lacan is regarded as a key influencer in bringing linguistics to Freudian psychology, by proposing that the unconscious is structured like a language; the effects of the unconscious are seen as breaks in language, in jokes, misinterpretations, slips, amongst others. Furthermore, language and signification are signs that point to, rather than signs that represent, our unconscious motivations (Oliver, 2002). His notion of subjectivity encompassed three main realms: the real, the symbolic, and the imaginary. Lacan's picture of the symbolic-real-imaginary orders are deeply rooted in Freudian notions of the oedipal phase, infantile sexuality, and the project of uncovering unconscious processes through language and associations (Lacan, 1977).

Although my training and practice is more aligned with the thinking of Melanie Klein, Winnicott, and Bowlby's attachment theories (see below), my knowledge of Kristeva's work has also clearly influenced the way I view the subject in language. As far as Kristeva is concerned, she was herself an "exile", arriving in Paris from Bulgaria during the height of the intellectual revolution of the 1960s, both embracing and challenging the ideas of intellectuals and colleagues (Moi, 1986). She was therefore acutely aware of the issues of loss and grief surrounding separation from the motherland and losing the mother tongue, describing herself as an outsider or "l'étranger". She also declared herself bereaved and grief stricken as her native language Bulgarian "became like a dead one", but going on to say that it came back to her in her dreams (Kristeva, 2000, p. 166). For Kristeva, however, being an outsider was an opportunity to look subjectively at language and form in a different way, challenging and going beyond the revolutionary ideas of the time, in particular in relation to the subject's birth into language.

Kristeva adopted and then extended Lacan's notion that, in order to become a subject and belong in the language, or the symbolic, it is necessary, first, to separate from that first object of which we are a part, the mother (Kristeva, 1984). This primary separation facilitates the ability to distinguish between self and "other" and between what is inside oneself and the outside world. It is, above all, language, and the process of naming, that seals this separation. Kristeva, however, goes a step further by suggesting that there are two separate modalities within the signifying process, namely the symbolic and the semiotic. The symbolic model includes those aspects of language which fall under the sign, the expressive communicative activity. The "semiotic chora"/realm is constituted by drives and those primary processes which displace and condense the energies of the body (Kristeva, 1984). For Freud and Lacan, the unconscious found its way into language through slips of the tongue, misnomers, and dreams. For Kristeva, then, the unconscious also finds its way into language through rhythm, semiotic fragrances, musicality, and perhaps in therapy, through the clients' physicality and silence.

What this chapter will also attempt to highlight is how the traumatised-exile-client requires more physical safety in the room, that is, the setting, the space, and, in essence, that the physical consistency becomes more important. Moreover, what has become evident in our work is that, for some of these extremely disturbed and traumatised clients who have only been awarded a year or sometimes two years of therapy, we have to limit the work and focus on providing a containing environment, a listening environment, thereby facilitating ego-supportive work.

I am focusing on two clients, both exiled in different ways, in this short piece while drawing on my own experience of exile, and my journey through this loss. I will talk about Jazmin, from Turkey, and Aliyah, from the border of Syria.

Jazmin: not using her mother's tongue

Jazmin was referred to our practice by her general practitioner, having previously received a short period of counselling at the GP's surgery, as well as several sessions of CBT through a local hospital. In her late thirties, she was on antipsychotic medication as well as antidepressants. Although she missed roughly a quarter of her sessions in the first year of the work, she completed the two-year contract and towards the end of the specified time expressed an interest in continuing with therapy— although she then did not telephone to book her exit interview. The written assessment itself was dominated by issues of separation and loss. The opening comment was that this "young woman was terrified of her panic attacks and felt she had been abused by her parents and husband". She was the eldest of five children born to parents from Turkey.

Her parents had fled political instability and potential persecution there and she and all her siblings were all born in the UK. They spoke both English and their parents' mother tongue at home. She told the assessor that she was completely estranged from her mother (who suffered from a severe and debilitating form of mental illness). I was immediately struck by the mirroring of Jazmin's estrangement from, and conflict with her actual mother and her "mother-land".

On meeting Jazmin, her physical presence had an impact on me and I found myself remembering many details about her appearance—she was an attractive, light-haired woman, with a pale face and large dark eyes. I was aware of my surprise at her light skin tone and hair, and thought about how we bring existing preconceptions and racial stereotypes about clients into sessions—she was Turkish, and therefore I expected her to have an olive skin! However, I believe that this was intrinsic to Jazmin, meaning the use of the physical to express what the symbolic could not allow her to say, and this became clearly linked to her difficulty with separation and attachment.

The sessions that followed, and many of those after it, were characterised by Jazmin's extreme anxiety, expressed in physical agitation, picking her skin on the top of her nose and tapping her face. She expressed her difficulty in being in the room through her tardiness and her missed sessions. By our fourth session Jazmin had already established a repetitive routine in which she made her physical presence felt in our space by trying to change the space when she entered:

> Jazmin walks in the door, dressed in a baggy black top and jeans. She puts her drink on the table and before sitting down she goes towards the window, sighs, and says, "Do you mind if I open this—it's very stuffy in here." She then struggles with the window, and invariably, I must stand up to help her.

Jazmin would then sit and pick at her hands and the top of her nose with a restlessness and nervousness that made me wonder if she was trying to feel where her body was. The jerky, out-of-control physical movements made it feel very much like being in the presence of a newborn infant just out of the safety and constraints of the womb and now uncontained by the mother. After six or seven weeks I raised with her the need to open the window, suggesting that we try to think together about what this might mean. Her response was literal, and she commented she "felt claustrophobic in small spaces". My attempt to link this difficulty on being in the room with me failed and she was unable to speak but reverted back to the physical touching and jerking and picking of her skin on her nose.

Jazmin was unable to bear my interpretation that her ambivalence about attending therapy was linked to her defence against any attachment or intimacy through the therapeutic relationship. This pattern continued in the weeks that followed: she was almost always very late, always very anxious, nervous, and distressed, and continued with her ritual of opening the window, picking at her skin. I think that an aspect of this was that she was struggling to remain in the room because she felt she was in the presence of a persecutory object. I refer here to Melanie Klein's object relation theories, whereby the infant in the early months of life suffers significant anxieties and defences caused by birth trauma, hunger, frustration, cold, etc. This experience results in what Klein referred to as the paranoid–schizoid position, the main characteristic of which is the splitting of the object (self and other) into good and bad, with very little or no integration between them (Segal, 2001). In this case, I am suggesting that the therapist becomes a "bad object" to the patient.

But was there more to this, I asked myself? Was this possibly a way of communicating her need to anchor herself physically, to use her control to change the room and make it her space, because she felt so exiled from herself? Did giving herself an imaginary "escape route", that is, the window, make being in the room bearable? I continued to facilitate this ritual as it was felt important that the sessions should be a containing environment for her, where I would reflect back and facilitate ego-supportive work.

In the weeks that followed, more was revealed about her past and about her relationship with her parents. A key factor was that her mother, who had experienced a very strict upbringing in her youth, had kept Jazmin captive in her bedroom when she was a teenager, to try to prevent her from going out with her friends and to parties. She was also prohibited from being with the family after dinner, and had to remain locked in her room. There appeared to be physical abuse as well.

Jazmin had finally seen the need to escape from this controlling and destructive maternal relationship and had run away to live with friends. Thereafter, she remained estranged from her mother, would not speak to her and would not use the language of her parents' homeland. Following her parents' divorce, she lived with her father, where she remained for the period of our work together.

After around six months Jazmin began to feel safer in the room with me—she was able to reflect and laugh at her "crazy rituals", like the route she took to her session. It was at this point where, having talked about it in supervision, I felt I had a sufficiently strong working alliance to make an interpretation about her defences and her fear of intimacy.

Jazmin arrives slightly late and immediately tries to open the window. She comments:

> "It's always stuffy in here," and stands up to open the window. She struggles with the latch but this time instead of helping her, I say:
> "I wonder if you need me to help you with this, because there is a part of you that needs me or wants me to take care of you? Perhaps this is difficult to acknowledge? But I also wonder if it is important for you to make this space seem safer, by changing it?"

I was also aware of the reality of Jazmin's experience, that she had experienced real captivity and I was able to wonder with her whether this also carried profoundly upsetting emotional memories. Was this room a mirror of the room she had been imprisoned in by her mother? Jazmin was tearful as she acknowledged this and said she was relieved we had talked about it. My acknowledging her unconscious fear, her difficulty, at a point when she was able to stand the interpretation, I believe, suggested that Jazmin was now becoming able to experience me as a more benign maternal object, and that some of her fear of my retaliation had subsided.

A result of this increased trust and degree of attachment, I believe, was that the sessions now became a safe place for her to deal with anger and resentment—a girlfriend letting her down, her lack of friends, and her father being annoying. We talked in supervision about how this was an important phase in her development—that she was in part testing me: was I the benign object who could bear her? But I did find myself becoming frustrated with her presentation of a life she loathed. There was also the overpowering envy of others which manifested itself in a longing to be part of a gang or a group. Regarding the envy, I think this was influenced a great deal by her unconscious sense of displacement. She talked about how she felt outside her peer group—her reality was that she had been locked up because her mother was trying to impose on her daughter her traditional restricted way of being separate from men until it was time to be married. However, I believe she felt outside the peer group as well, psychically, and this became clearer as the work continued.

During this period, I thought especially about my own countertransference: my frustration and irritation in particular, my lack of clarity, and an overwhelming sense of failure and sadness. What was Jazmin lodging in me? What was she giving me, leaving me to carry, when she didn't come to her sessions or when she dumped her negativity, especially her verbal hatred, into the room when she split off the "bad" parts of her life, projecting them into others? In our sessions, she spoke in English, which was not her mother's mother tongue, and her hatred poured out of her with such vehemence, almost violence. I felt myself reeling.

Living in another language

Although it was clear that my feelings were the result of projective identification, I was surprised at the strength of them (while projection is perceiving someone else as having one's own characteristics, projective identification is a more active process where one gets rid of something belonging to the self into someone else (Hinshelwood, 1989). Segal describes it as "evoking in someone else aspects of the self which one cannot bear" (2001, p. 36). I thought about my own exile and journey through analysis and how I had felt completely silenced by my own loss and fear. I wondered if my identification with Jazmin, also separated from her family and an outsider among her peers, was making me feel more of a failure in the work and whether her traumatic loss of a mother was affecting the way I worked? I thought about this in supervision and with my own therapist. Jazmin's suffering was multilayered, and it seemed to me that she was carrying many painful emotional memories. It began to become clear to me how important it was for Jazmin to feel heard, acknowledged, and listened to. I needed to show her that I was not a rejecting maternal object, and that I could bear her anger and rage.

The clear cultural conflict between the old country, the mother's strict upbringing focusing on modest behaviour, and the new country with the youthful desires of a typically "British" teenager occurred on a psychic level. In his paper "Migration Loss and Memory", John Clare writes, "When people have to get away, for whatever reason, exile can be the quest for a potential discourse in another place in another language" (Szekacs-Weisz & Ward, 2004). He continues, in relation to Beckett on his self-imposed exile: "In French, Beckett could begin to achieve the separateness and freedom from his mother's savage loving which nothing else had made possible" (Casement, quoted in Clare, p. 185). It did seem as though the parent's loss and anguish in their exile from their mother-land had become their daughter's psychoanalytical one and I believe that Jazmin needed to exile herself from her overpowering and controlling mother (she was now physically estranged from her). In using English in the therapy, Jazmin was able to separate herself from her mother's "savage loving" by using another language and this gave her access to her hateful feelings which she poured on me (Clare, p. 185). Before going on to think about this more, I would like to consider another patient and exile, Aliyah.

Aliyah: using the second language as retreat

Aliyah was born and grew up near the border with Syria, but she came to the practice with the request that she work with someone for whom English was their first language. This was thought a great deal about in the assessment supervision session as we felt that the comment was rich in material about the client's relationship with her mother tongue and motherland—we understood that it reflected a need to stay separate from the "other" country of her past, and to reinforce herself in the UK.

The details of the assessment and the information gleaned from the early sessions contained much brutality and cruelty. Aliyah had grown up in the family of the rejected first wife of a peasant farmer. There were several stories about beatings and emotional deprivation with favours being given to the younger second wife and her children. Early on in the work, she told me she had been sexually groomed by a married man whom she had met through a sibling as a very young girl; in fact when she was yet to reach her teens. Their relationship had dominated her early life, as a child, then as a student and adolescent, and it continued to affect her now as a parent. She sought asylum in the UK whilst in her twenties and was employed as a domestic worker, sending her money home to "the man" (he was never named throughout the two years of our work) who had groomed her in a form of sexual slavery. The story she told was shocking and sad as it seemed as though over time the man and his family were able also to come to reside in the UK, and Aliyah lived for a time as his second wife, working extremely hard to support both families while having two children with him. The parallels between her and her own mother trapped in poverty and rejected in her relationship were painfully obvious. However, throughout the duration of our work, Aliyah was estranged from and at odds with the man and she gave me every indication that she despised and hated him. She supported herself whilst at college and had been working in industry but this had proved too stressful for her as she had been constantly in conflict with many of her colleagues and finally her employers.

When I first met Aliyah I was struck how small she was, physically. However, rather than being overwhelmed by a quite large consulting room, it was as if her entire being took over the space. She spoke extremely loudly and it was as if she needed everyone to be aware of her. Although it was sometimes extremely tiring being in the room with Aliyah, I was always aware of an enormously powerful sense of sadness. This was more poignant when I discovered that her relationship with "the man" and her having his children had resulted in her being disowned by her family and she had been forbidden by her own siblings to make any contact with her aged and ill mother. In this it seemed her exile was complete. But what an impact this physical and psychic exile had had on this client.

Aliyah tried to create a "typical British lifestyle" for her family and spent money and time manically booking a variety of shows and events for them. She would also book the children into club after club, after school and at the weekends. This had two functions. On the one hand, I believe she felt she was giving them opportunities she did not have, and that this would repair the damage she had suffered though her parents' neglect and poverty. The other function was to limit the time she spent in their presence, because this in itself was extremely overwhelming for her. However, after about six months it became clear that Aliyah had really come to therapy because of her fear of her anger and the damage it was doing to her children. She saw herself as a truly damaging and frightening object. She would sit with her head in her hands, shaking her head and weeping, saying over and over again, "I am so terrible, I am such a terrible mother."

As in the case of Jazmin, it was necessary to facilitate ego-supportive work with this disturbed and damaged client and provide a safe containing physical and emotional environment: the therapy was time-limited and the sessions weekly. Her suffering was deep, layered, and extremely painful and the countertransference was exceptionally powerful in the room. The depth of her loss struck me when she told me that she would not speak her local dialect to "the man"/the "father of her children". "No, I must speak English to him," she told me. Here I could see and we could think together how separating herself from the language of her abusers made her feel safer, and more in control, and was a way in which she could separate herself from the pain and rage she felt. But I wondered how hard that must have been, separating from the mother tongue because it felt symbolic of the abuse and, I suggested tentatively to her, actually abusive using it. She was initially unable to think about this, dismissing it, but I would find that the comment had resonated somewhere within her unconscious. She came to her session once more distraught that she had "lost it again" at breakfast with her child. We examined her anger and her grief carefully, gently, and she was able to locate it in her past, in her childhood, at her breakfasts when she was being screamed at and abused. Over time she came to see that she was acting out her own unresolved anger and her grief and her overwhelming self-disgust on her children. This was important, but this did not necessarily help her stop her aggressive behaviour.

Aliyah's vulnerable moments resulted in flooding, outpourings of details and dramas of her everyday, present life, followed by weeping, rocking, and a physical shrinking. I believe that the flooding became a way she could keep herself in the here and now, because her past felt too abusive and traumatic—her past was full of memories of her rejection as the unloved child (of an unloved wife), teen, and adult. However, the flooding was also her way of keeping any attachment to me at bay (the depth, length, and the extent of her verbal attacks made the sessions very tiring). It was also a way that she unconsciously forced me to stay in the room with her and listen to her, and when she could not speak she expressed her fear and rage and despair in her regressed physical rituals to her audience, me.

An added complexity was that Aliyah's children were the result of, and symbolic of, the abuse she had experienced and the reason for her to remain in contact with her abuser. I do believe that this affected her greatly, unconsciously—ultimately it was the source of unimaginable rage and hatred and it became clear to me that she was terrified of this anger towards her children. When she was especially disturbed, either by herself or the children, she would stop speaking altogether and revert to a form of self-soothing, rocking, touching herself, and repeating phrases under her breath. That she was able to do this reflects that she had found in the therapy and therapy room a safe space and place. During these moments, I found that I needed to listen carefully to and acknowledge Aliyah's difficulties, and her suffering in the room, even if it meant repeating myself and there was no acknowledgement of what I had said.

After a period of absence from therapy due to a work commitment, Aliyah walked in and told me she had been in contact with the local social services about one of her children who at eleven years old had attacked her and threatened suicide. It saddened me that she had not been able to attend her sessions to get the help she needed, and I acknowledged this to her. She continued by telling me that the child had been referred to a psychoanalytic unit for assessment and she, Aliyah, would also require an assessment for therapy. As our time was nearing its end, I felt that this would be a natural way forward. I felt strongly that, for Aliyah, whose safe world was always on a knife edge through the presence of "the man", the structure of therapy and the safety expressed by the therapy room was extremely important.

After she had completed the assessment, I was telephoned by the institution, and the analyst who had made the assessment suggested she was not sure they would be offering any sessions to Aliyah as they were concerned that she would be unable to "use" the therapy. I did not agree. We had a conversation and I made my recommendations. Aliyah had so many deep wounds and so many layers of suffering. Had I noted changes in her behaviour, a sizeable shift in her as a result of the work? What I can say is that for two years Aliyah experienced a positive therapeutic listening. She was seen, and she was heard, her case was heard, her fears were heard in the safety of the therapy room. We had acknowledged her loss and her exile and the pain she was in. No matter how aggressive and angry she became, I was always the same, and I was always there and she could not destroy or damage me. Winnicott coined the phrase "good enough mother" to describe the most basic mother–child relationship and it is based on the premise that the "good enough mother" will provide an environment which will facilitate healthy emotional development in her baby. Here the mother actively fulfils her baby's need for emotional warmth and love, protecting the child from physical and emotional danger. Over time, the baby and the mother who are "one and the same at birth", with the mother "processing the baby's feelings", begin to separate and develop a sense of "me" and "not me" (Winnicott, 1965), with the mother gradually adapting less to the infant who in turn is able to deal with her failure.

In the case of Aliyah, I believe in her therapy she had experienced for the first time a maternal good object and a good enough mother. Perhaps that is just about good enough for someone exiled from themselves.

It's at this point then, I would like to return to Jazmin.

Jazmin: silence at birth

Throughout the therapy Jazmin had expressed a fantasy that she and her father would go to live in their homeland Turkey, where she might find a nice local man to be her husband. After she had been seeing me for about a year she told me that she and her father had planned a "scouting" trip with a friend but the friend pulled out of the trip at the last minute. The decision was made to go ahead with the trip despite this. The trip was not a success. Below is an extract from the first session on her return.

Session 41

J: It was awful, dreadful. I thought it would be different. I didn't feel at home and I couldn't stand it there. I should never have gone just with my father. I just feel so depressed when I see all those people sitting in the hateful sun.

The following week

J: I am so glad to be here. This week has been terrible. I need to get out but the sunny weather is so depressing. My dad is depressing and annoying.

What struck me was the dramatic shift in Jazmin's attitude to the sessions: she now appeared desperate to attend and she was on time. It was as though the recognition of her own need had been unlocked. Her somewhat manic rejection of her father was also apparent in her constant references to him as "depressing" and "annoying". Her references in the session to the weather and the sun outside seemed to have been aroused by the trip to their homeland, where it was sunny. I thought about the link between her former identification and fusion with her father and this recent development: the rejection of the father and the father/motherland.

In the following session, Jazmin and I thought together about the weather and why it oppressed her. She claimed it was that it reminded her of her loneliness and her lack of a partner. I suggested to her that this had somehow been highlighted to her while she was away: perhaps she had wanted to feel part of her family there, and was disappointed she had not. She became increasingly agitated, and kept repeating that she shouldn't go away on holiday with her father, "I should have had some friends with me," and admitted that she hadn't wanted to go out and that she had "just wanted to come home". I felt that it was important for Jazmin to be contained in this moment of distress as it seemed as though an important, almost oedipal, milestone had been crossed, that she no longer unconsciously wanted to be the loved object of desire of the father or fused with and attached to the parent, that she wanted to be separate from him (Spurling, 2009, pp. 46–59).

Separating from the father went in tandem with her desire to find a replacement male object and this happened very quickly. Within two weeks of returning, Jazmin met Olly. She arrived one morning to our session and seemed more than usually agitated. She described how she had gone to a party and had met this man Olly, to whom she was instantly attracted. She had her mobile telephone in her hand, and kept glancing at it. She started talking quickly about how they had met and had ended up kissing all night. She had been in touch with him since, and was going out with him that evening. I commented that it seemed difficult to separate herself from her phone/Olly and I also tried to help her think about what it might mean for her to bring the phone into the session. This was too difficult for her to think about at this time, such was her anxiety around Olly, so I found myself reflecting instead on how difficult it seemed to be in the room and we thought together about her anxiety.

The relationship moved very quickly and Olly became an obsession. Within three weeks of meeting him, he became the central focus of her life. He seemed to be quite the kind of man she had always fantasised about, but never imagined would like her. She described him as a "gang leader", a kind of "hard man", with tattoos and aggression. From a cultural point of view, he could not have been more different from her father. He had spent time in prison; he had a "gang" of men and women with whom he spent a great deal of time. Many sessions were spent talking about what had attracted her to him, both during and after the relationship ended. (Once the relationship was over, and after she had worked through him being a denigrated and hated object, she could see that he had represented something alien or foreign to her, both culturally and emotionally and that this had been an intrinsic part of the attraction.)

Jazmin was unable to bear separation from Olly. She would call him up to fifty times in the first hour of the day, but it soon became clear that Olly had begun to find her behaviour oppressive. She was told to stop calling him constantly, or he would break off the relationship. She was allowed to call him only twice a day between 4 and 8 pm. This was as painful to witness as a drug addict giving up heroin. She would sit in my room wringing her hands, in a terrible state of anxiety, and thinking only of when she would be calling him. The following two months of the therapy followed this pattern, with Jazmin in a near catatonic state of anxiety over whether Olly was in love with her or not, waiting for his calls, waiting to see him. During this time Jazmin attended her sessions regularly, and did not ask for the window to be opened. I provided a supportive and reflective role, reminding her several times that this was a safe place for her. When the relationship finally ended, Jazmin was desperate, but also relieved that her agony was over.

Together, we talked about her relationship with Olly and she was able to see how the thought of the relationship was more important than the relationship itself. She also was able to identify in herself the need to project the idealised man onto Olly, and could see that the power balance in the relationship had been out of kilter due to her own lack of confidence and self-worth. We also spent a lot of time in the last five months of our work together talking about her attachment to Olly and her early attachment memories. We talked about how it did not seem possible for her to trust that Olly would hold her in mind when they were separated, just like a toddler learning to separate from her mother might think that the mother had abandoned her, and that she would not come back.

It was during this period that she remembered that her parents had told her that she cried a lot when she was a baby, and that they had placed a mattress over the cot to muffle her sounds. This was a very painful memory, and Jazmin was able to verbalise the sense of rage she felt, and we tried to think about the significance of this: of what her parents were unable to bear in her when they imprisoned her and how that had affected her ability to make attachment bonds.

It may be useful here to make reference to the work of Bowlby. Bowlby began with the premise that the infant is born vulnerable to his or her environment and therefore is dependent on caregivers for survival. This results in the infant, and, in time, the young child, creating an attachment bond with the carer (Bowlby, 1979). With Winnicott, Bowlby determined that it is these early relationships and the way our attachment figures respond to us that determines our capacity to relate to others in a healthy way (Winnicott, 1965). The way in which the child develops a belief that there is a secure base from which they can be separated and to which they can safely return determines the kind of attachment (secure/insecure; anxious; ambivalent; organised/disorganised) they will have and will develop in future relationships (Bowlby, 1979, pp. 126–160).

Because of Jazmin's anxious attachment (Winnicott, 1965), I had to remind her numerous times of our time limitation and in the last few months she was able to be annoyed with me because of this. We discussed how it was important that she was able to express this and that I was able to stand it, so she could see that her damaging and attacking self could be borne, in the way that as a baby, I believe, it could not. For when Jazmin had been silenced in her cot, she had been brutally separated from her maternal object and placed in exile from the mother.

This early and brutal separation had created a premature sense of unbearable loss and facilitated the psychic exile she felt, which I believe in turn led to her attachment difficulties. Knowing this had helped me to understand Jazmin's pain and fear, both at not being heard in the sessions and in obsessive behaviour during her relationship with Olly. The physical and mental abuse she had suffered and the loss she experienced—her own and that which was projected onto her by her parents through their cultural alienation—instilled in her such great fear and pain that she struggled to develop a sense of herself. I think she existed in a state of constant alienation and dissociation, in exile from a true self.

Yet I do believe that Jazmin found through the therapy a place safe enough to release the pain of this silencing. She was able to reduce her anxiety medication over the course of the therapy. Finding employment in the last two months of her contract indicated to me that through the therapy she had begun to identify an internal good object that was not controlling or withholding or silencing and one that could bear her damaging and attacking self.

Conclusion

I began this chapter talking about exile and loss and my own struggle with this grief, which silenced me. We have seen that for the traumatised client in exile, language can become a major obstacle to self-expression and health. Through the therapy sessions with Jazmin and Aliyah, I have also attempted to highlight this wordless space, looking at how silence, together with movement and repetition, can be a way of unconscious communication when language fails. In exploring this with clients who are also in exile, we can see that the mother tongue can sometimes be a hindrance in expressing primitive feelings and, as in the case of Aliyah, a second language is used to express anger and despair. What we have also seen is that in Jazmin's family, where the exiled parents are unable to bear their losses (of homeland, family, and language), the cries of their baby who is separated from her mother (her primitive mode of communication) prove too much for them and they must silence her. The infant's crying, and her pain becomes a metaphor for theirs. This premature and brutal separation of the infant from the mother, and the fact that the infant receives the projections of the parents, has significant psychic repercussions for the infant.

Both silenced and rejected, Jazmin and Aliyah must use another language which is not the mother tongue to communicate because the language of the motherland is also the language of the abuser. Sometimes, this other "language" is not verbal, but rather has a physical, even musical, alphabet which involves rocking and drumming, and repetition of movement. This is sometimes what the therapist needs to listen to; not only what is not said, but also how it is said in physical form. In this sense, it is worth revisiting Kristeva, who experienced first hand the trauma of the exile. For her, language fails to express the unconscious, and we must look to other "breaks" in language, such as silence or rhythm, or what she calls a "repetitive sonority" which she sees as a "thrusting tooth pushing upward before being capped with the crown of language" (Kristeva, 1984, pp. 28–29). Listening to trauma, as I hope I have been able to demonstrate in this chapter, means listening beyond language: it may require us to listen to the parts of the patients' discourse that is not verbal and it may require us to ensure that for those who are also exiled from themselves, their physical safety is utmost in our minds.

References

Bowlby, J. (1979). *The Making and Breaking of Affectional Bonds*. London: Routledge, 1989.

Clare, J. (2004). *Getting Away from the Mother Tongue: Samuel Beckett and Psychoanalysis*. In: J. Szekacs-Weisz & I. Ward (Eds.), *Lost Childhood and the Language of Exile* (pp. 182–192). London: Imago.

Hinshelwood, R. D. (1989). *A Dictionary of Kleinian Thought*. London: Free Association.

Kristeva, J. (1984). *Revolution in Poetic Language*. M. Waller (Trans.). New York: Columbia.

Kristeva, J. (2000). *Crisis of the European Subject*. New York: Other Press.

Lacan, J. (1977). *Écrits: A Selection*. A. Sheridan (Trans.). Boston, MA: W. W. Norton, 1987.

Moi, T. (1986). *The Kristeva Reader*. Oxford: Blackwell.

Oliver, K. (Ed.) (2002). *The Portable Kristeva*. New York: Columbia University Press.

Segal, J. (2001) *Melanie Klein*. London: Sage.

Spurling, L. (2009). *An Introduction to Psychodynamic Counseling*. Basingstoke, UK: Palgrave Macmillan.

Szekacs-Weisz, J., & Ward, I. (Eds.) (2004). *Lost Childhood and the Language of Exile*. London: Imago.

Winnicott, D. W. (1965). *The Maturational Processes and the Facilitating Environment: Studies in the Theory of Emotional Development*. London: Tavistock.

CHAPTER FIVE

Outre-mer et la langue de ma mère

Monique Morris

> *"It is not our purpose to become each other; it is to recognize each other to learn to see the other and honour him for what he is."*
>
> Hermann Hesse (1930)

I had and still have a French accent and come from Paris. When I first arrived in London, I experienced a sense of confusion, which included the fear of the unknown and at the same time a sense of freedom. Was this sense of freedom a dream, an illusion?

I was born during the war in 1943. Paris was still occupied by the German army. Almost all French civilians were undernourished due to the rationing and shortage of food, which I believe had a great effect on the French psyche. I grew up in an atmosphere of fear, resentment, and prejudice. The occupation of Paris had an impact on many Parisians including my own family.

My father was born in Paris and lived with both his parents and a younger brother, who, I believe, died tragically in his early twenties. My father was a cultured and educated man who sadly became addicted to a life of drinking and gambling, and my mother was often left looking after all three of us. He also lost his own father before he married my mother. She was under eighteen while he was twelve years older. I was born a year later.

My mother was born in Paris, she was the third oldest of seven children. At a very early age her parents immigrated to Algeria where she lived with them until the age of three or four. I have very little knowledge of my mother's family life in Algeria, or the reasons why they left France. One of her sisters (three years older than my mother) came back to Paris, followed a couple of years later by my mother. Their aunt and paternal grandmother respectively brought them up. They lost contact with their own parents, sisters, and brothers.

Following many years of tension and disturbance in a very difficult marriage, my mother left my father, and we were all sent to different boarding schools. I was eleven years old. My boarding school was a Catholic convent run by "les Soeurs de la Sagesse" ("The Sisters of Wisdom"). My experience of boarding school was difficult, and I missed playing with and looking after my two brothers. I was too angry with my parents to miss them.

"The Sisters of Wisdom" is an interesting name, as, by having this new life forced upon me, and perhaps acquiring my own "wisdom", I became almost silent in the world of adults and very noisy (often playing the clown) in the world of children. The adult world could not be trusted!

I left boarding school aged fifteen and went to work in Paris as a secretary and lived on my own for several years. Life in Paris in the late 1950s and early '60s was exciting, and I spent several years observing and discovering a new world, spending time listening to jazz in various cafés in the Latin quarter, meeting new people, new families all from different backgrounds, religions, and countries. I was trying to exorcise the nuns and, perhaps unconsciously, my family.

Thus, when I met an English man who suggested I come to visit him in London, I did not hesitate and decided to spend a few weeks there. I was yet again transported into a new world. I was intrigued and curious and felt that a new door was opening in front of me. I decided to stay.

My new life began, and I eventually married this man. He was not only English but, as important, Jewish. This was not surprising, as I was already interested in Jewish culture and history, and many of my friends in Paris were Jews, some from North Africa. I was still searching for something different, something I could belong to.

I decided to convert to Judaism before my marriage. I sincerely believed that I had fully adapted to and was adopted by this new country, new religion, and new family, and had at last found some stability. I was beginning to find another voice in this new language, which seemed so much more powerful to the point that I was forgetting (or repressing) "la langue de ma mère".

On my occasional visits to France, I was often told that I spoke French badly and that I had an English accent. I soon began to realise that I was no longer French in France. I had lost my French identity. At the same time, despite my determined attempt to integrate fully into my new life in England, I could not be English either. Who was I? Where did I belong? Had I become an outsider in both languages?

Everyone has an accent, and attitudes towards accents are often based on social connotations and prejudices surrounding the location or social group associated with that accent. I often felt, though, that people had difficulties in categorising me in a social group because of my accent.

For many years, and still today, when meeting new people, I am often asked: "How can you choose to live in London? Paris is such a beautiful city." Or "How long have you been living in England?" which leads to "You still have a very strong French accent!" As a young mother, when I opened the door to a caller I was often asked, "Where is the woman of the house?" They took me to be the *au pair* or *la femme de ménage*.

Parisian women and their accent seemed to be perceived as sexy and exotic, so people tend not to see who you really are and associate the way you speak as a reflection of your personality. One may think that sounding sexy and glamorous is a good thing; that is, until you have something important to say and nobody takes you seriously.

I had and still have a French accent and come from Paris. This was all true, but I was in a very different dream-like space. I certainly did not feel like this sexy, glamorous woman, nor could I understand why Paris stood in such an elevated place in the imaginations of English people. At the same time, and because of this idealisation, my newfound home felt denigrated by these same natives. My opinion of life in England seemed to be far higher than theirs.

I often had to defend London, and still do, the city I now love, where I felt I could discover something new, exciting, and creative in a language that allowed me to find my own voice. This was in marked contrast to my earlier years, growing up in Paris, where my education was formal, strict, and rigid, leaving little space for creativity and imagination. I still have vague childhood memories of sitting at a desk and having to learn through fear and obedience, never allowed to question any authority figures. These experiences often left me feeling paralysed and unable to retain the information, which was apparently the object of the exercise.

Looking back at my journey I am reminded of the Greek legend about a young sculptor named Pygmalion, which inspired George Bernard Shaw's 1913 eponymous stage play based also on the Cinderella story, which led in turn to the famous musical *My Fair Lady* (1956). Pygmalion was a talented young sculptor in Cyprus who had strong misgivings about women. He was determined never to marry, believing that his commitment to his art was enough to sustain his passions. However, one day he began to carve a statue of his ideal woman. He was determined to form the image of the perfect woman, embodying every feminine grace and virtue.

The statue grew more impressive each day. When he finally completed this beautiful work of art Pygmalion realised that he had fallen passionately in love with it. He began to treat the statue as if it was alive and he would kiss it, embrace it. Soon Pygmalion became desperately unhappy, for his lifeless, cold stone statue could not respond to the warmth of his love and his desires. He had only succeeded in creating his own frustration and despair. I suggest that to some extent we all sometimes behave like Pygmalion. Many of us are attracted and often impressed by "the idealised other". In my case I had carved my own symbolic statue, represented in the form of a new language, a new country, a new family, new friends.

I think of myself as someone resilient who can adapt easily to new situations, and have tried to remain positive and optimistic about the world around me, so I had to master this new language to settle in my new life. Quite quickly I learned to speak English fluently, although not necessarily grammatically correctly and certainly with a strong accent. I began to settle in this new life.

When my daughter was born, I was in some kind of euphoria. I could not sleep for hours and hours after her birth, looking at her, admiring her, thinking "How could this miracle happen?" and was I capable of giving life to someone else? I did not know then that I still had not given life to myself!

At first, I spoke French to her and sang French nursery rhymes, but very quickly, it became too difficult for both of us. I think we both needed to be part of the community in which we lived, and although my daughter understood far more French than she admitted, she soon began to refuse to speak it. Was she unconsciously in tune with my own ambivalence?

When my son was born nearly three years later, I was no longer speaking French with either of my children. I now feel sad about this, both for my loss and theirs. However, both my children do now speak two languages. My daughter's second language is French, spoken with an English accent, though I believe not as strong as my French accent. In addition, my son after living in Israel for several years speaks Hebrew! Are my children, somewhat like me, hovering between their country of birth and the "other country" of second language? Do they need to belong to two countries? But it is not for me to make assumptions as it is, and will become, their own personal narrative.

I was invited to attend an open evening at my daughter's first year in primary school. She seemed anxious about my visit. Before going to the school to meet her teacher she gave me a set of instructions: "Please mum, can you just listen to the teacher and not speak, and can you wear a shirt and a skirt like all the other mums!" I suddenly became acutely aware of her embarrassment. I was different to the other mums!

Both of my children would often (and they still do at times) make fun of my turn of phrase, my accent, my mistakes and would respond to some of my demands accordingly. For example, when I used to tell them to go upstairs and did not pronounce the s at the end, they would go up one step and await the next set of instructions. I was often teased and imitated on the way I spoke by my family, friends, my children (of course Peter Sellers has a lot to answer for!). Although I was irritated at the time, I know now that it was meant with affection. My two grand-daughters, too, seem to take great delight at times in imitating my accent, which has provided us with another intimate private space with its own language and accent that enabled us to play and laugh together and per-haps not take ourselves too seriously.

To my surprise, my adoptive country gave me the opportunity to study, which I do believe would not have been possible in Paris. I had the chance to study for a degree, which was not easy. I had to work on my written English which, unlike the way I have learnt to speak, I learnt intuitively rather than formally. I finally qualified and worked as a social worker. As a social worker, I occasionally encountered some difficulties with my accent and the accent of others, especially on the telephone when the helpful non-verbal aspects of communication were missing, as well as having to decipher other people's accents.

However, after working for several years with families, I started to realise that some of their pain and difficulties were all too frequently insoluble. I began to feel a sense of frustration and, at times, despair. I realised that I needed to explore these feelings in more depth. It was then that I decided to enter the world of psychoanalysis. I could not change the suffering and the inequalities of the world, but I might be able to make sense of my own frustration and despair.

A few days before I embarked on my long analysis, I had this dream:

> I was in a café in Golders Green sitting outside on the pavement with my mother. Although I knew that I was in Golders Green, the street and the café resembled far more a Parisian café in Montparnasse, and I was confused. I had to go and pick up my social work qualification from a supervisor from a Jewish agency where I worked in my final placement. I told my mother to sit and wait for me. I think I felt very proud of my achievements. I managed to speak and study in a foreign language! I rang the doorbell several times, but they would not let me in. I insisted. Finally, my supervisor came to the door and told me that she could not let me in. I was very distressed and said:
> "But I need my certificate."
> Her reply was:
> "You cannot come in because you are ill and need treatment."
> I was devastated and very confused.
> I went back to the café where I had left my mother. I was in tears and very distressed. I told her what had happened and her only comment was:
> "I don't know why you thought you could change; I have always said that you could not do it!"

What a gift for my forthcoming analysis! This dream illustrates also my confusion and ambivalence about my two countries. Was it possible to change? I believe that my attempt to build a bridge between my place of birth and my new life in London was in its infancy. I needed my mother's approval, but more importantly, I needed to go back to the beginning. Did I hope for a return towards "la langue de ma mère", my fantasy of an early experience of her warmth, her body, my birth?

It was during the years of my analysis that I began to return to France regularly for holidays. I believe I was looking to find the possibility of finding some intimacy with family and friends. But I realised that "the French" again teased me in my own country. I spoke French with English intonations, what they called "Franglais". My accent was often mentioned. I did feel at times upset and frustrated by discovering that what I had lost and left behind in leaving Paris was part of my identity.

One of my patients, whom I will call Nicole, came from France. She encountered many difficulties moving from one country to another, especially with learning English and with her accent. She left France at a similar age to mine when I left France. I very quickly developed a strong identification with her. When Nicole contacted me, she wanted to speak her maternal tongue. This made me anxious. After all, my studies, training, my own analyses had been conducted in English. However, I also realised that I needed to take up the challenge, as it was vital to my own journey and my work with all my patients.

Nicole often commented on my house: the consulting room, the furniture, she said, could only belong to someone English. I was only pretending to be French! The development of the negative transference was almost instant. Nicole has always been successful at school and had a very strong formal education. She is and always was a high achiever academically. She has cultivated her French accent, as she seems to have no interest in the English language and no desire to make her life in this country. In her social and professional life, she has surrounded herself mostly with French people, Spaniards, Brazilians, etc. Furthermore, for several years she has felt that I was trying to stop her returning to France.

She has now begun to make sense of her strong attacks on me. At last after several years we entered into a much warmer and understanding relationship. She no longer denigrates either me, or her life here in London. She is able to move back and forth between France and England,

and appreciate what London offers her. France is no longer viewed as the perfect country. I believe that my willingness to tolerate her attacks enabled her to develop the trust needed to accept the reality of being in England and let go of her fantasy of an idealised France.

In the legend, as it turns out, the goddess Venus is moved by Pygmalion's prayer and she takes pity on him and brings the statue to life. Pygmalion and Galatia (the name given to his statue when she came alive) were married under the goddess' blessing (Ovid, 8 AD).

In contrast to Pygmalion, Eliza, in *My Fair Lady* (George Cukor film, 1964) is a girl who was born and grew up in the dregs of society. Her transformation is almost unrecognisable; she becomes a highly regarded and perfectly acceptable lady. She had no longer any trace of an unacceptable accent, or should I say, "an acceptable accent". Had Eliza become a woman of desire, another ornamental statue among the upper social classes? Her tragedy eventually became the loss of her desire, the loss of her love.

In this chapter I have shared my internal and external attempts to integrate my two worlds while mourning what I now feel I have lost. I doubt now that I will ever lose my accent, nor would I ever become Eliza and take elocution classes, and of course now I believe that my persistent French accent was the only way I managed to retain my roots despite myself.

References

Hesse, H. (1930). *Narcissus and Goldmund*. London: Peter Owen, 2006.

Ovid (8 AD). *Metamorphoses*. London: Penguin, 2004.

Shaw, G. B. (1913). *Pygmalion*. London: Penguin, 2003.

CHAPTER SIX

Silence, dissonance, and harmony: integrating the multilingual self

Cédric Bouët-Willaumez

Introduction

In this chapter, I would like to tell the story of the research on the multilingual experience in psychotherapy that I carried out as the final assignment for my psychotherapy studies. I will illustrate that the conclusions of this research are as important as the personal journey I took to reach them. I have found both equally valuable and I hope that by showing how they inform each other, I may give the reader some useful bearings for their own reflection on the topic of this research.

The hypothesis that I wanted to test in my inquiry was that therapists who have a multilingual background manifest different aspects of their self when they practise in one of the languages that they know, and that this has an effect on the therapeutic relationship.

What may nowadays seem like a statement of the obvious felt, at the time that I formulated my hypothesis, like a "eureka" moment. I had undergone five years of training without tuition on this particular subject. I had had therapy and supervision in English for six years, and had been practising exclusively in English, without so much as a thought to the fact that doing all of this in a second language may be something that deserved close attention. As I will explain later, I had only looked at second language practice from a concrete and practical standpoint. I felt that merely increasing my mastery of the English language would take care of things.

Choosing my research topic was not at all straightforward: I remember jotting down quite a few ideas, growing quite irritated and then putting my pencil down in frustration. Then, I stopped searching for things and let the inquiry "choose me" (Hiles, 2001). My hypothesis seemed to form spontaneously in my mind.

This experience marked the beginning of my research—it was also something that I chose to forget as, once again, I shifted my focus away from what was happening in me towards what was going on outside.

Old friends and foes

Indeed, what seemed to matter most when I started my research was to make good. I was aware that I had left unattended two languages that I knew: I didn't practise in French; I seldom spoke with my family; and I generally avoided French speakers in London. As for Dutch, it was all but relegated to my unconscious. I did not feel at peace with this, and I suspect that this is why I unconsciously set myself up to go well beyond what was needed for an academic exercise.

Dutch is my mother's first language, and the only one of five which she speaks without an accent. It is the language in which I pronounced my first words, and it was the language that she and I spoke until my brother was born, months before I turned four.

French was my father's language, the language of my family, my friends, and of the country I was born and raised in. It was the language for outside, for other people. Dutch was shared with my grandmother and mother only, while French was shared with a multitude that I was thrust into when my mother tongue was no longer spoken at home.

It was years before I understood that some kind of battle had been fought and lost: my father didn't get on with his Dutch mother-in-law, my mother's only family in her country of birth, and generally loathed the Dutch. My mother must have tired of defending her corner and retreated. My father dropped out of our regular gatherings in Amsterdam, and the family was split along a north-south divide until my grandmother passed away when I was twelve years old. My mother did not take me or my younger brother to her funeral, so that we wouldn't miss school. It was as if my grandmother had vanished as France gained full custody of her grandchildren.

In the years that followed I made an effort to keep the Dutch language alive. I took it for my baccalaureate, and later studied for a term in Rotterdam where again I took exams in Dutch. But after graduation and my military service, the career that beckoned was to be in France, and in French. I experienced an impoverishment of my person and became progressively estranged from both parents.

After two years of unfulfilling work and minimal family life, I was offered an opportunity to go to study music in London. I made up my mind on the spot and left as fast as I could, without a thought. In fact, I never *decided* to leave for England; it was as if I had rolled over in my sleep, fallen off Paris, and landed in Acton.

When I started reflecting on this time of my life, I saw that language seemed to be both the mould and the voice of my experience, because it manifested and organised it—split it—at the same time. I had experienced a weightiness and a gravity, an impoverishment and depersonalisation that manifested in the dark and elaborate language of my father, and an experience of a doomed closeness that found its expression in Dutch, the language of a child determined to deny the reality of his loss.

It seems now I felt that growing up would have meant abandoning the relationship with my mother, and that by moving to England I chose not to grow up but to carry on playing. I turned down the volume on the inner conversation between my two voices until it became silent, and engaged with music and English.

Happening upon my research hypothesis, I decided to make good and turned up the volume on this conversation, hoping to make sense of what would come to my conscious ear. I actively sought to practise in French, which I soon did, took up supervision in French and joined the MLPC. I also started a conversation with my mother in Dutch, which we agreed would start off in writing to make up for my considerable loss of oral fluency.

As I mentioned above, my intention was to *re-animate* relationships with languages: I am choosing that word because it means both to revive and to lend soul to, as Julia Borossa puts it, "a corpse which remains warm" (2004, p. 30). I wanted to be alive in all my three languages, and to undo the effect of the apparent neglect that had left them withered and undead.

As I immersed myself in my inquiry, I analysed my experience and found that it felt uncomfortably and expectedly familiar: I enjoyed my skill in French but was wary of certain words and turns of phrase, which would reveal my speech impediment. And in Dutch, I witnessed my mother's enthusiasm and dedication to help me resurrect the language but somehow I felt I needed to be forgiven for something bad I had done. After all, Julie Kristeva says, "not speaking a mother tongue is matricide" (in Borossa, 2004, p. 30). In French, I saw skill hiding awkwardness, and in Dutch, abundance spoiled by guilt.

Unlike the English language, neither French nor Dutch afforded me uncomplicated and completely rewarding experiences. It was as if the conflict between my parents took expression in my experience of their languages: not only did French and Dutch seem pitted against each other; it felt as if they were attacking the other from within.

I became aware that I had resurrected old enemies.

Father's voice, mother's body, and resistance

At the same time, I undertook secondary research, hoping to find material that would help me organise my immersive experience as I went along.

I found little—in fact, it was a good forty-five years after the publication of the studies on hysteria by Freud and Breuer that Emmanuel Velikowski made the first contribution to the subject by stating that a recently acquired language could become a language for the unconscious (Amati-Mehler, Argentieri, & Canestri, 1994).

I will not present theory in great detail, and mention it only as it relates to actual examples from my practice and my interviews with fellow therapists. I have changed biographical details where appropriate so that the anonymity of patients and interviewees is protected.

What I knew from previous practice was that, as Stengel (Amati-Mehler, Argentieri, & Canestri, 1994) states, the emotional relationship between a word and what it represents for the individual will vary according to the language in which the association occurs. For example,

Mohan, a British-Indian patient who was four years old when his father was excluded from the family because of alcoholism, was very affected by his lack of relationship with him. He would tell me, in crude terms, that the word "daddy" meant nothing to him. I asked him to utter the word in his mother tongue, as he used to, and when he did, he found to his great surprise that this provoked a strong emotional reaction—an emotion that had been repressed since "papa" became "daddy".

But what struck me the most in my discussions with fellow therapists was the common theme of resistance: indeed, half of the people I interviewed expressed feeling a resistance to practising in their mother tongue. Invariably, the first motive they identified for their resistance was the need for mastery. One said: "It's almost as if therapy was a sub-language" and commented that, should they ever practise in their mother tongue, they felt like they would need to learn to speak again. Lack of practice of their native languages left them feeling less fluent and more vulnerable. In fact, the issue of mastery was the sole conscious concern for all but one of the therapists I interviewed, which was very much my own position before the initial engagement with my inquiry.

Further discussion revealed that this resistance was motivated by a desire to keep safe the sense of the identity that they had developed in their second language. One therapist, Maria, told me that moving to the UK and taking up English as her language of choice had for some time been tantamount to "deleting" her past completely.

She recalled working in English with a patient of the same nationality as her, who had lived in England for forty years and spoke English perfectly. Maria resented the fact that her patient would, from time to time, pick some words from their common mother tongue, and ask personal questions. She told me that her patient "did not have a clear understanding of boundaries". Maria knew that her countertransference reaction was to resist this woman's attempts to get things out of her, because she had "always given her mother what she wanted".

I could interpret Maria's experience using theories by Greenson (Amati-Mehler, Argentieri, & Canestri, 1994) and Stengel (ibid.). It seemed that in learning a new language, we create a new inner representation of our mother, which coexists with the one that was formed earlier. These are important contributions which however do not address the physical reality of how we come to acquire an inner mother-image that is rooted in, and therefore manageable by, language.

Katerina's experience was quite illustrative of this missing aspect in the theories I had read about so far. Katerina, who has been in England for more than half of her life, was describing how she felt she would perform as a therapist in her mother tongue. She wanted to tell me that because of her lesser fluency and somewhat reduced vocabulary, she would be less tactful and gentle in holding her patients, but she made a slip and substituted "tactful" for "tactile". She saw that the resistance that she felt towards her engagement with her mother tongue was linked to the bad experience of not being held appropriately when she was a child. We could see a confirmation of this association during the interview when, upon my request, she spoke aloud in her mother tongue and had suddenly felt, to quote her: "ungrounded and uncontained".

More recent research by Boysson-Bardies (2001) tells us just how close to mother's body language is. Boysson-Bardies explains that it is the mother's voice that the unborn infant hears, amplified by mother's body and filtered from the outside by the abdomen and uterine walls. The musical envelope of mother's speech is preserved well enough, along with almost a third of the phonemes, to enable the baby to respond to structured speech in different languages and, for example, to express a preference not only for mother's voice, but to a specific poem read by her during gestation and after birth, and to her language.

As for the earliest months of life after birth, Alan Schore (2003) explains that the dynamic, two-person affect regulation through non-verbal cues formed the basis from which babbling and articulate speech emerged. This allows me to suggest that there is an unbroken continuity in the experience of relatedness as it is manifested in the earliest vocal productions, then babbling, then speech and its development into languages.

On this basis, we can say that learning a second language can be considered as an attempt not only to create new inner images and emotional relationships with them, but also to redefine our means of *experiencing* the world, and primarily, our mothering. Referring to people who have experienced trauma in a given linguistic context and learned a second language later in life, Edith Buxbaum (Amati-Mehler, Argentieri, & Canestri, 1994) says that this depth strategy allows multilinguals to keep things "unreal". I hope to show that the domain covered by the mother tongue remains very real indeed, even if it would seem to lose importance and agency in the second-language speaker. I particularly like the formulation offered by a therapist who said, in relation to verbalising trauma in another language, that it is: "a bit like running down the street to your friend's parents' house and saying: 'My parents aren't being nice to me'".

The antalgic posture

My experience of interviewing Adil is an illustration of the fact that in the multilingual therapist, different language-bound domains remain related.

Adil practises psychotherapy in English, a second language that he masters perfectly and speaks without an accent, as well as the language of his country of birth, formerly colonised by Western powers. When I asked him about his experience of working in these two languages, he replied he didn't feel that there were any psychological factors affecting him that were linked to either language. He said that he practised in two languages so that he could work with two different social groups who had very different experiences: indeed, people from his home country had lived under colonial rule and had suffered in a series of civil wars. This offered him an opportunity to work with people whose personal dynamics were often defined in relation to the experience of powerlessness and the trauma of war and the struggle for independence.

We discussed how it felt to be working with such a patient group, and contrasted this with his experience of working in English. With his perfect mastery of the English language, Adil told me that he felt that he was "beating the enemy at their own game". It emerged during our interview that working in his native tongue brought about a set of feelings quite opposed to that, because it allowed him to get in touch with feelings of powerlessness and frustration that were also quite central in his life. He had not been aware of this. Through our discussion he deduced that his bilingual practice was a means to separate opposed experiences of power and powerlessness. They were contiguous in his unconscious and split off from each other in his practice. His choices meant that he could have both "places" (his parents' house and his friends' house) without experiencing confusion.

I found that this strategy was central to managing trauma. As said earlier, using a second language is a means of cordoning off traumatic memories, and preventing associations that could lead to the trauma resurfacing.

Adil's example seemed to show something more complex, and more interesting: he was willing to work in a language that he associated with traumatic experiences of powerlessness, on the unconscious condition that he could compensate for this with an opposing experience of power. He had found an unconscious balance between good and bad experiences.

This reminded me of what French psychiatrist Boris Cyrulnik (1997) called the "antalgic posture", "antalgic" meaning "going against the pain". The antalgic posture is a subtle and often unconscious rearrangement of body posture to accommodate an injury. For example, when I broke a piece of cartilage in my knee I developed a gait that rendered the broken cartilage "non-functional" and prevented pain. But doing this affected my spine and meant I eventually had to have knee surgery.

An antalgic posture makes it possible to minimise the pain from an existing wound, but this is not without consequences: the pain is not directly experienced as itself, but as the imprint it leaves on the "healthy" part of the body. I saw from what I had learned from my colleagues that this work could be read in the way that people carried themselves, and in the choices they made.

Using the antalgic posture as a metaphor, I looked back at the strategies that I had seen described—and lived out—in my interviews, and asked myself: "If the choice of language can define a whole new experience of the world, how do the old and the new coexist?"

Maria, who had wished to delete her past, always kept a strong accent, and came to accept herself as a foreigner. She knew she "wanted to be seen hiding". Adil had found a way to balance experiences of power and powerlessness in a way hitherto unknown to him, but which could be read from the in-depth discussion that we had.

As for me, I did not check myself for a limp.

Making good—an attempt

However, I was keen to spot a limp in Paula's gait when I interviewed her. Paula was a practitioner of psychosynthesis, who was born and raised in Spain to a Spanish mother and Swedish father. Her father left the family—and the country—before Paula's birth, and she and her mother developed an extremely close and exclusive relationship, which Paula increasingly viewed as intrusive. Her absent father was only ever talked about in negative terms, and her mother forbade her from learning his language. Paula left Spain for the UK as soon as she turned eighteen. She then embraced the English language as a means for her to live and own a sensual and emotional experience that was distinct from her experience in Spanish.

Paula told me that the English language had become "a third". For her, the use of a language had the power to affect a person's experience. She explained that she would make tape recordings of all of her sessions and listen to them afterwards, not so much to analyse their content, but to appreciate how she sounded. This "third", invested with affect and sensation, was a way to compensate for her lack of a triadic relationship. To quote Pina Antinucci-Mark (1990), this was "a transitional space" in which she would be able to manage some of the unresolved and ambivalent aspects of her relationship to both parents.

During her interview, we discussed her work with an English-speaking patient, which had spanned more than three years and had ended some time before. She explained that she had encouraged her patient to consider language as a malleable object that he could adapt to his needs, and to create idiosyncrasies and neologisms. A small subset of the English language, a sort of limited therapeutic patois, emerged for them to use.

Paula explained that as the therapy drew to a close, two things happened. First, the subset of made-up terms and expressions was gradually "decommissioned" and replaced with mainstream English—Paula told me it needed to happen because the words of the patois had been losing their affective charge. Second, Paula encouraged her patient to prepare for the end of therapy by thinking about his life and the challenges ahead as a therapist would. This seemed to be effective and her patient reported that he had also found it a "freeing experience".

Paula felt that, at the same time as she was gently reintroducing her patient to the outside world and reinforcing his autonomy, she relinquished the usage of what had afforded both of them an exclusive and intimate experience. She saw this as a way to gently let go of him.

However, it also appeared to me that, when she noticed that the made-up language was losing its distinct intimate quality in the relationship, Paula had made this patient "take her inside him". She helped him to organise his judgement and agency around internalisations of her, which were closely associated with the made-up language, which, from being public and shared, would become private. This relationship to language was very similar to the one that she had developed for herself.

It looked like Paula needed her patient to go through an experience that was a controlled and gradual version of her own. In her life, she had created her "third" as a way for her to deal with the issues presented by her unboundaried twosome with her mother and the complete absence of her father. She had, however, needed to make a clean break from her mother by changing countries and adopting a new language. In this patient's therapy, Paula encouraged him to create a "third", separate from the outside world, that she could share with him. She related to this "third" in the same way. For her patient, this turned the therapeutic space into a foreign country, and their "therapeutic patois" into a foreign language.

However, this approach meant that she encouraged her patient to imitate her own internal structure, with her as an internalised helpful and benevolent figure.

I felt that Paula's story was consistent with the second part of my hypothesis, namely, that the way that therapists managed the inner polarity of their self through the use of language had an impact on the therapeutic relationship. Her inner rift lay between her father and mother, between her experience of outside and inside, the wondrously alien and the stiflingly familiar. Her desire to heal was projected upon the relationship and her patient adopted her polarity, and her own antalgic posture.

Should traumatised people necessarily face up to their traumatic memories, so that they may heal? Cyrulnik (1997) suggests that we could usefully compare denial of trauma with the reaction of a car-crash victim who, when he manages to find an antalgic posture, refuses to be moved when help arrives. He explains that in doing so, the motorist is right because if he is touched carelessly his wounds might get worse. But he is also wrong because he cannot be saved if he is left alone on the roadside.

Paula eventually chose not to stay by the roadside and only a few years ago went to visit her late father's country of birth for the first time in her life. She described with some emotion how this had been a healing experience for her.

Meanwhile, I chose to stay on the roadside.

Acting out

When I formulated my hypothesis, it naturally became an object to study and a reason to focus externally. As I mentioned in my introduction, and again just now, I did not take heed of the way that the research question had come to me, but rather focused entirely on what was happening in front of my eyes, while neglecting to check in with myself on a deep enough subjective level.

At the time that I started seeing Alice, my first French patient, my life took a turn for the worse.

I had left my full-time job as a mental health worker in a residential crisis centre to concentrate on developing my private psychotherapy practice, but found that it didn't develop like I needed it to and quickly experienced serious financial difficulties. I wrote to my mother—in Dutch—that I had to leave my current flat and would need to stay at a friend's for a while. She replied—in French and in no uncertain terms—that my projects had not worked out and that I should consider returning to France and getting a job there. This remains the only piece of correspondence I ever tore up. Our relationship became silent once more.

I will go back to what those circumstances meant to me, but for now I want to mention them just as a background to my work with Alice, the first ever French- speaking patient I treated.

Alice would tell me she had no memories of her childhood. Or more precisely, that her first childhood memory was also the last: an eight-year-old child, she is standing next to her mother, facing her father. It is late at night and her parents should be in bed but her father is wearing his coat because he is about to leave the house. His wife is begging him tearfully not to go away and, pointing to Alice, cries: "You could at least stay for her!" Her father left on the spot and never returned.

From this moment she was effectively made to bear the burden of the responsibility of her parents' divorce. She recounted this tragic scene without any emotion. Alice's mother subsequently entered a depression, which lasted for years until she remarried. Then, her depression not only seemed to evaporate, Alice explained. It was as if it had never been there, and she became angry with her mother for her obstinate optimism and good mood.

What Alice wanted most was another relationship: but she put it in terms that indicated a desire to unlock something within her first. She did not bring her ex-partner to the sessions in a manner that would make him a living, three-dimensional being. Instead, she referred constantly to her own "flow". Alice had a strong physical and emotional presence, and enjoyed physical activity and exercise because it would bring her body in focus in a compelling manner and block out her obsessive and self-attacking thinking.

I put it to her that, more than a new partner, she wanted her mental life to take on the simplicity and fluency of her physical body, and the immediacy of her emotions. Although she agreed with this, I felt as if she and I were not making progress. Her obsessive preoccupations lost some of their power, but I would find myself unable to facilitate the exploration of her earlier life.

The gilded cage

I brought Alice's case to my French supervisor, and associated freely around my ambivalent experience of mastery and ineffectiveness in Alice's therapy. I felt that the French language was my gilded cage, from which I could not escape to reach out to Alice and give her what she needed. At this moment I spontaneously visualised Abdallah ...

Abdallah is a character from *Tintin*, a classic comic by Hergé with which French children had been growing up since 1930. He bears some resemblance to Dennis the Menace. Abdallah is the eight-year-old son of a wealthy emir: he is an inarticulate, selfish, mischievous, spoilt brat. Abdallah's billionaire father is the only parent featured in the comic and his mother is not mentioned.

I felt that Abdallah perfectly embodied the way I felt about the French language, and what I expressed when I spoke it. He had great wealth and power, and yet was a motherless, inarticulate, and angry child, a prisoner of his father's huge palace. I felt as motherless as Abdallah—my mother had become a foreigner again when she prompted me to cut short my experiment.

I understood that from my position in life, I could not possibly offer Alice what she needed, because I felt as bereft as she did. For both of us, a whole piece of childhood had become silent. Alice's mother was acting as if separation, depression, and her daughter's childhood never happened. She didn't take ownership for the separation from her husband, which was something that Alice chose to do. And by suddenly adopting a language foreign to us both, my mother had repeated an earlier pattern, which had split off and frozen four years of my childhood. Neither my mother nor Alice's wanted to keep a live connection to the early relationship with their children, leaving them to hold projected feelings on their behalf. For both Alice and me, the projected feeling was guilt.

And quite importantly, neither of us could find mother's body.

Sinking or swimming in the consulting room

Once I understood this, I felt that I held evidence that the inner conflict I lived through in the opposition between language-bound experiences affected the therapeutic relationship.

And importantly, I understood that my inquiry into the theme of multilingualism was actually as old as I was. It had been unconscious for thirty-six years, it became conscious when I formulated my hypothesis, and I proceeded to act it out when I focused on what was going on outside.

I had found an explanation for my lack of progress with Alice. I had summoned up an experience from childhood through my immersion in the languages that I knew then and I had come to a position similar to the one which I held when I was four years old. The coping strategy I adopted to manage the conflict born out of an impossible choice—father or mother—was to silence the sound of the clash at the border. In speaking French, I came to silence the voice that longed for mother, and to resent the voice that belonged to father, and to impede my own speech.

Speaking French with Alice under these circumstances, I could only offer a therapeutic space that reflected this inner split. In my opinion and experience, and to quote Anthony Lunt, "It is not the therapist's knowledge or supposed knowledge that cures his patients but his way of being with them" (1990, p. 31)—and my way of being was split alongside a line materialised by language. I could not model an inner space of harmony. Without me recognising the similarity of our experiences, we could not move on.

I wanted to re-animate all my languages at the same time, and to experience life through the broadest spectrum possible to me: what resulted was cacophony. My mother had ultimately resisted my attempt to resuscitate our early relationship, and I responded the same way as I did thirty-four years back. I have indeed already explained that because I could not find my mother anymore, because she had become a foreigner, I felt as if I didn't have a mother at all and it affected the way I was with Alice. What I have not yet explained is the link between my precarious material situation at the time of my inquiry, and an experience I had around the time of the birth of my brother.

A month before I turned four, in February 1974, I was playing outside on the estate where my family lived. My mother was watching me from the window of the second floor of our building. I managed to evade her attention long enough to follow one of our neighbour's children, who was eight years old, to the estate's uncovered swimming pool that was just around the corner. Health and safety in those days can't have been what it has become now because we got to the pool quite easily, and after daring me to take the plunge, he pushed me in. I flailed briefly on the surface, gave up and sank straight to the bottom. The rest of this story is the stuff of family legend, because I was quickly rescued by a passer-by who was hurrying to a business meeting but had become hopelessly lost on our deserted estate. He caught a glimpse of bubbles breaking the surface of a silent pool and dived straight into the ice-cold water. It took quite a bit of therapy for me to accept that my near-drowning had not been an accident.

More than thirty years later I reacted the same way—losing my connection to my mother, I let myself sink and hit a metaphorical bottom. I also recall the setting I offered to my therapy patients at the time. It had been inspired by R. D. Laing's reported way of setting up his sessions, as Anthony Lunt, a former patient of Laing's for several years described to me in conversation. I liked arriving without my belongings, without a watch, settling in a room that I had not yet worked in that day and which I had not prepared, letting the patients enter first and choose a seat so that I could set my position according to theirs. I offered my patients the experience I had had in the swimming pool: being pushed in, flailing away, and being met by someone who didn't belong there—or anywhere.

I found that this free and uncontained set-up greatly favoured the emergence of unconscious material that was related to experiences of transience, displacement, and instability. I also realised that some patients needed a more evidently predictable container, and that my own all-out attitude towards my inquiry set no clear and firm boundaries for my patients. It proved ultimately too unsafe for two of them. One of them, as she was about to end her therapy with me at short notice, told me: "I feel undone." There is no doubt in my mind that my patient was expressing what was happening in my life, which I had unconsciously transferred to the therapeutic space by acting out my inquiry.

Then something happened in my work with Mohan, a patient I mentioned at the beginning of this chapter, which only became clear later. One session, he didn't feel like using the reclining chairs we had sat on for months and chose an upright chair, which was quite a bit higher than mine. I stayed in the reclining chair, and almost instantly, Mohan became confused and scared. I tried to explore this feeling with him but my efforts did not generate insight. He came back on the following session with a look of panic on his face and explained that he needed to stop therapy with immediate effect. Again, I could not help him gain insight into this quite spectacular change of heart: he had seemed very committed to his therapy until then.

I am still unsure of what exactly prompted his hurried departure. But it is, however, quite clear to me that on that occasion I changed my attitude to psychotherapy by claiming my own space and not adjusting my position to my patient's. From this session onwards I prepared rooms, took up my bag, wore a watch, and always used the same chair. Mohan was not prepared for this: I had not worked with him from a fixed, solid position. The flexible set-up of the therapy made me a potential rescuer and I believe that he might have thought that by giving up this flexibility he would risk drowning.

Conclusion

The title of this chapter is, in a nutshell, a description of my inquiry. I chose the English language as the sound of my inner silence. When I listened in, I heard the dissonant choir of my father and mother tongues. Because my inquiry was only partly conscious, a large part of it was acted out, and quite spectacularly so.

C. G. Jung (1962) said that it was inevitable that unconscious material should seek to manifest itself outwardly, and that the individual personality was also driven to evolve out of its unconscious conditions so that it may see itself completely. I believe that if we have more than one language at our disposal, and because of the sheer power of language itself, we will use *them* to experience ourselves as a whole, but that we will do this unconsciously; I learned from my inquiry that we do this as soon as language is part of our experience.

I suggest that in taking up such work, preferably as part of psychotherapy, as a patient or as a therapist, we render conscious a personal inquiry that is as old, and as important, as we are. Therapy is the conscious effort to break the silence and experience dissonance, and to let our languages manifest greater harmony together.

The price of silence is enduring discomfort, and as therapists, this impacts the effectiveness of the encounters we offer to our patients. The price of the inquiry is dissonance and discomfort, and I would suggest that the prize is harmony. What does harmony sound like? I can only speak from my personal experience because, to keep the musical metaphor, we all have different orchestras playing. But the feeling that I have about this is that it can only exist when all the musicians become aware of each other, of their range, timbre, and part, and of the watchful conductor, which is our conscious mind.

References

Amati-Mehler, J., Argentieri, S., & Canestri, J. (1994). *The Babel of the Unconscious*. Madison, CT: International Universities Press.

Antinucci-Mark, G. (1990). Speaking in tongues in the consulting room or the dialectic of foreignness. *British Journal of Psychotherapy*, 6(4): 375–383.

Borossa, J. (2004). Languages of loss, languages of connectedness. In: J. Szekacs-Weisz & I. Ward (Eds.), *Lost Childhood and the Language of Exile*. London: Karnac.

Boysson-Bardies, B. (2001). *How Language Comes to Children*. Cambridge, MA: MIT Press.

Cyrulnik, B. (1997). *Sous le signe du lien*. Paris: Hachette Littératures.

Hiles, D. (2001). *Heuristic Inquiry in Transpersonal Research*. http://www.psy. dmu.ac.uk/drhiles/HIpaper.htm (last accessed 8 December 2020).

Jung, C. G. (1962). *Memories, Dreams, Reflections*. New York: HarperCollins, 1995.

Lunt, A. (1990). *Apollo versus the Echomaker: Laingian Approach to Psychotherapy, Dreams and Shamanism*. London: Vega, 2002.

Schore, A. N. (2003). *Affect Regulation and the Repair of the Self*. (Norton Series on Interpersonal Neurobiology). New York: W. W. Norton.

CHAPTER SEVEN

Return to Berlin: my forbidden mother tongue

Edna Sovin

For a long time I have hesitated to write about my own experiences; it seemed to me that it had all been said before. There is already such a large and growing literature by and about Holocaust survivors, refugees, hidden children, and those who came to Britain on Kindertransports. My own bit of history does not add much to earlier accounts. But perhaps my individual version of how that history affected my development, and what I have learned about the transmission of trauma from one generation to the next, may be worth sharing.

I found that, in preparing this account, my thoughts built up in layers. One of these is the historical narrative, as I learned it from the beginning of my life, through the versions of events as told me by my parents and other authority figures. The second layer is my own reconstruction of the same events, as I learned to trust my own experiences and perceptions. And finally, there has been the development of meaning, as I have observed my own processes over time. An important part of that process took place around the age of sixteen years, and thereafter in and out of therapy, over more than forty years.

My parents were perhaps like the majority of refugees who did not talk of their experiences during the bad years of the Nazi era. Like most others, they just got on with rebuilding a reasonable life. In the 1980s, forty years after the end of World War II, it was noticed that some of these people who seemed to have coped so positively were beginning to show signs of trauma. As they approached retirement age, and they were no longer focused on raising families, they could not keep their experiences walled off any longer. This led to the establishment of organisations like the Raphael counselling service, Shalvata, and the Holocaust Survivors' Centre. Soon it became clear that the descendants of these people had been left with a bewildering legacy, and they came together and eventually founded the Second Generation Network.

During my childhood and adolescence, I was often told that I was a very lucky girl. And it was, of course, absolutely true. I was never hungry, cold, or homeless. Nor was I ever exposed to abnormal levels of cruelty or terror. I was only eight months old when my parents fled Berlin in April 1938. We were allowed entry at Croydon airport because we had just managed to get transit visas, on the understanding that when some more papers arrived, we would join my uncle in New York. Without those visas we would have had to go to Ulan Bator, in Outer Mongolia— the only alternative we had at the time.

Some of our extended family also managed to get out before the start of the war and were scattered to the four corners of the world. My maternal grandfather had died in 1936. The three remaining grandparents and many other relatives were left behind. They suffered years of increasing hardship and misery, loneliness and persecution, until they were rounded up and deported to concentration camps. My maternal grandmother and others who were well-known outside Germany, and some other relatively lucky ones, were sent to the camp of Theresienstadt (or Terezin) in Czechoslovakia. Many of them, especially the frail or elderly, died of starvation or disease. Others were selected for deportation from there to Auschwitz where they were murdered. When the war was over, my maternal grandmother, my father's aunt, and a couple of cousins were still alive.

My father's parents had disappeared. Only recently I realised that I had the right to ask, and that I needed to know, what had happened to them. At the Wiener Library the information was immediately available—all that was needed was that I ask for it. I found that they had been deported to Riga, and "*verschollen*", meaning destroyed.

I am now at about the age my grandparents were in 1942, when they were deported. But I am here. I live with my excellent husband in a warm house, in a friendly neighbourhood, with as much of material comforts as I could wish for. I have raised three great children to adulthood, I have good friends and a satisfying profession. I really am lucky!

But something has puzzled me for some time. My closest friends are all dynamic, energetic people. They are creative, enthusiastic, and engaged. They don't seem to feel intimidated by anyone, and they are open to all kinds of experiences. They seem to have a lot of fun. And this even applies to those of them who have had really very painful or traumatic childhood experiences.

I see myself as very different. Relatively speaking, I see myself as slow-moving and inhibited. I have often been preoccupied with my health, and I am anxious about many aspects of life. I do have bursts of enthusiasm and active involvement in life, and times of pleasure and even of joy, when I think I have found people or an organisation where I feel welcome, where I can be at home. When I can feel part of the group, as of right—then I think, for a time, that my years of living on the margins, or being a tolerated outsider may at last be over. However, quite often this has ended in bitter disillusionment and flight. Then I am back to being an outsider, and this has frequently been followed by a period of depression. My years of personal therapy have helped with the recognition of what I contributed to my own suffering. But some questions remained unanswered.

Perhaps, "because I am lucky", several things have happened that have helped me to begin to make some sense of my history and how it has affected me. The latest of these events was being asked to write this chapter. Working on this text has in itself created a stream of ideas and new meanings. I became aware that some of the most interesting points, especially those relating to loss, caused me pain. For some time, I could not really understand it.

The event that stimulated much of my recent process of making meaning of my feelings came in the form of an invitation to Berlin in May of 2019. I was invited to unveil a plaque in honour of my maternal grandparents. The invitation came from a Jewish feminist group, which had been researching the lives of influential Jewish women from before World War II. The first plaque had been in honour of Regina Jonas, who in 1930 had become the first woman rabbi in Germany.

My grandparents were the second in line for recognition. I learned that my grandfather was a teacher and lay preacher, very involved in religious reform within Judaism. My grandmother was an early feminist. She was president of the Judischesfrauenverein, that is, the Jewish Women's Association, founded by Bertha Pappenheim—Anna O to Freudians. Grandmother was also the first woman member to take her seat in the Jewish Assembly.

To my surprise, substantial groups of officials and interested people were involved in celebrating my grandparents' achievements. Berlin government representatives, leaders of the Jewish community, television crews, and the press turned out for the unveiling. As I talked to my audience about the personal background to these public figures who were being honoured, and the story of the survival of my family up to the present day, I was struck by the strange feeling that the story seemed interesting and meaningful to many people from around the world. I enjoyed my "fifteen minutes of fame", seeing my visit reported in the *Jewish Chronicle*, and being asked by women from several countries if they could publish my talk on their websites.

I had asked my husband not to come with me on this trip, which sounds unkind. But I wanted to feel free to speak German. If he had been there, all those we met would have used English instead. And I did enjoy using my first language—my mother tongue. Nevertheless, I did not feel competent to give my speeches in German but spoke in English with a translator. Although I can speak German reasonably well, I am quite illiterate. However, as on two earlier visits to Berlin, I felt alien, unsafe, and I couldn't wait to get out of there!

I would like now to explore how my relationship with German has been formed, and to see how this is connected with my development into the person I have become. Woven in with this question is another. When my parents died, I could not cry or feel grief. On reflection, this also seems to be connected with the peculiarities of my upbringing. So, I think I will give you some more history.

Having arrived in London in April 1939, we did not have long to settle in. War broke out in September, and by early 1940 the *Daily Mail* had whipped up such hysteria about the threat enemy aliens posed that Churchill sent out an order to "collar the lot". We were rounded up and sent to the Isle of Man, where areas of the capital, Douglas, and other resorts had been turned into prison camps. We were there for two and a half years, very pleasant years for me. I was "lucky" in being safely housed in a hotel by a lovely beach, with both my parents, and plenty of other children to play with. Meanwhile the poor London children were having to hide in shelters during the first Blitz.

Until recently, I thought of myself as learning to speak after arriving in England, and therefore having English as my first language. But as I was exploring this time in my life, it occurs to me that, from the time we got here, I was always with German-speaking people, and this would have held true until we came back to London in 1942, when I was about four. This realisation has made sense of some early memories of that time, which had puzzled me. One was of being lost in the Kilburn High Road. I got separated from my mother, and I was crying for her. Some kind shop girls took me into the storeroom at Woolworth and tried to find out what was wrong. I remember one of them saying that she knew there were some "foreigners" living in a big building nearby—and she quickly took me back to my frantic mother.

Soon afterwards I was in the playground of the school next door. I was sitting on some steps when a couple of little girls approached and spoke to me. I remember being unable to understand them, and shaking my head sadly, and they went away. Now it is clear that by the age of four, I was still struggling with English. A little later, I was out with my parents, and began to talk. They whispered urgently that I must not speak German in the street. People wouldn't like it—because England was at war with Germany. It seemed to be a matter of life and death.

We moved to North London, and when the second Blitz began in 1943, my father took me to Shropshire. He explained that all the children were being evacuated from London to get away from the bombs. We had already spent some nights huddled on the coal stacks in the cellar. Mother had gone to work earlier that day, and I don't remember saying goodbye to her. But I do remember taking hold of a previously neglected doll and clutching her tightly all through the journey.

It was probably around this time that I remember the first occasion when my father, usually quite affectionate towards me, spoke to me in a deep, fierce voice, with a stern, scary face, saying: "Jetzt musst du ganz furchtbar artig sein!" ("Now you must be terribly well-behaved!") Again, it seemed to carry the implication that this was a matter of life or death.

And I understood that this good behaviour was connected with not being a crybaby, not making a fuss or irritating people. In other words, I was not to show any distress I might be feeling,

My father left me for six weeks with a nice family in Wellington. There was a beautiful school set in green fields, and lots of children to run around with in the countryside. Then my parents came and took me away, and on to another foster family in Birmingham. I don't remember any explanation of why I could not stay in Wellington. I suppose I had been there on some kind of "transit visa" too. In Birmingham, I was fostered by a young English widow with a son just two or three years older than me. This was arranged through people my parents had met in the internment camp, who lived on the other side of the road. As I remember it, it was on my occasional visits to that house, of that well-settled Jewish family, that I first really felt what it meant to be unwanted, just tolerated out of some obligation.

Otherwise, Birmingham retains for me an impression of sunshine and fun, of freedom of movement, and a very kind but unemotional mother figure who was not anxious or overprotective. And above all, I was not an only child, but had a regular companion.

With my foster-brother I could walk to and from school, play with the local children in the nearby fields, explore a heavenly bluebell wood in the spring, and share a traditional English Christmas in his grandparents' house.

It was probably soon after I arrived in Birmingham that I declared that I would not speak German any more. It was the hateful language of the enemy, and from then on, I would only speak English. Away from my parents I was happily identifying with the mainstream English culture around me. So, at five and a half, the language of my parents, of affection and intimacy, had become something shameful. I was not able to make the distinction at the time. But I think my sense of shame extended beyond issues of war, to foreignness, that is otherness, and that this included what little I then grasped of our Jewishness.

My parents had to have permission to leave London. One or other of them would visit me for a few hours once a month, and I don't remember being especially pleased to see them, or of missing them when they left. As I try to remember, what comes back to me are confused impressions of their presence reconnecting me with the "not belonging" experience.

Each month they would "blow my cover". And, as well as being ashamed of their otherness, I may have been struggling with my shame at wanting to escape the implications of our relatedness.

As the war drew towards its end, my parents brought me back to London. So far as I know, we never had any further contact with my foster family—although I have found one letter that my foster-brother wrote to me soon afterwards. Leaving people behind, without a backward glance, just seems to have been the way things were done. Lot's wife turned into a pillar of salt when she looked back at the destruction of her home, and Orpheus lost Eurydice forever when he looked back as they were trying to leave the Underworld. I am doing a lot of "looking back" now—and I have to hope that enough time has passed for it to be survivable.

I remember a recurring dream I had of seeing my foster-brother at the corner of our London street. I ran to him eagerly, full of joy, thinking that I was not forgotten after all, and that he had come to see me. But he was scornful and cold. He and his mother were visiting old friends in another house and had no interest in me at all. I think that I had that dream quite often, but never got it to end differently. As an adult I asked my mother why we had not stayed in touch with my foster family. She could only say that "That's just how things were," and quickly changed the subject.

Initially, London at the end of the war was exciting. The bomb sites gave children a new territory to explore, and wonderful stuff to collect, like putty and pieces of chandeliers. Then there were street parties and going to the Palace to cheer the royal family with the huge crowds on VE Day.

But as the excitement died down, I was back in grim, grey London, where my parents did not like me to play in the street, and anyway, they were suspicious of the local children. They held themselves aloof from even their Jewish neighbours. They only seemed comfortable with a small clique of refugee couples, most of whom they had met during internment. And in this restricted social group there were no children. I have known many other only children, but they all had extended families who were an active part of their lives. It is hard to convey how lonely I often was. From eleven onwards I was sent off to camp in the summer holidays and would live in a state of manic excitement for the two golden weeks, until I had to come home, when I was often very low-spirited until school began again.

I believe that the worst effect of not having an ongoing secure peer group was that there was no counterweight to my parents' world view, or to the picture of our family situation that they gave me. Gradually, my parents rebuilt their lives. And as I settled down at home, I began speaking German again. My mother was a doctor and became one of the first GPs in the new National Health Service. My father slowly built up a small business. They bought a house and a car and had foreign holidays. They were not religious, but joined their local synagogue, as that had been obligatory in Germany.

This was another source of confusion for me. We were Jews. My mother suggested that her family had been quite enthusiastic about it. My father openly scorned and hated orthodox Jews and wasn't going to let any stupid dietary laws interfere with his love of ham. But it was made clear to me that one should be married and buried as a Jew, and that it was my duty to keep up this tradition. God didn't come into it. Even more confusing—they had a warm friendship with one very orthodox widow and her family. She lived very close to us, and the relationship had been forged during the darkest days of the Blitz on a basis of mutual support and lasted for the rest of their lives.

Later, when in my thirties, I decided to join a Reform synagogue and began to attend services and get really interested. My parents treated me as having gone slightly mad. They hoped I would get over it soon. But I was beginning to find my own voice. This had started when I became a counsellor with Relate, and a few years later when I trained as a psycho-analytical therapist. I began to question many assumptions. My father could be a kind, generous, and warm person, and he had many talents. But he was also domineering and controlling. We were never allowed to challenge his view of the world. He could not tolerate talk of anyone else's achievements. Ambition was ridiculous and also dangerous. It was important for Jews to keep their heads below the parapet. My mother's only area of autonomy was in her work, and she kept her professional life going until she dropped, when she was nearly eighty.

Mother was always very anxious about my physical health. I had been premature, and skinny, and she had wept at the sight of my matchstick fingers. Throughout my childhood she worried that I was developing muscular dystrophy or rheumatic fever. Any aches and pains led to consultations with specialists. I learned that the way to get my mother's attention was to be unwell. Psychic pain had to be somatised. When I had a young family, and was developing outside interests, I might sometimes complain of tiredness. Then my mother would remind me, "You are not very strong, and you must be careful not to take on too much." So far as I know, there was no real basis for this, but I am still struggling against this injunction.

At the very end of his life my father once, and only once, spoke of feelings of guilt about leaving his parents behind. Although, as I told him, he had tried all he could to rescue them, he said, "I should have tried harder." Our near addiction to being ill had many determinants. I also wonder whether it was a way of diminishing our survivor guilt. I suspect that my family culture of being ill or depressed is also a way of not being fully alive; of hanging between the world of the fully living, and that of our lost dead who cannot be mourned. There are just too many of them, and a whole world in which they once existed that is gone forever.

When my mother died at eighty-one, I took possession of a large hoard of crumpled, discoloured, and strange-smelling letters and documents, which she had thrown into a drawer and left. This was all the correspondence between my parents and their own parents after we left Germany, until the deportations. And even more significant for me was a pile of letters written by my mother's mother after she was taken from Theresienstadt to Switzerland, when she was seventy, and frail. While she waited for a visa to enable her to come to Britain or America, she wrote copious letters all round the world.

I was fascinated by the wonderful personality that came through in the correspondence. But I got a real shock when I found references to myself. She wrote of her pleasure in getting my letters and drawings, and commented on my school reports, and said how much she looked forward to seeing me again. I could read her post-war letters because they were written in English. Grandmother wrote in the first one that, after all that had happened, she would not write German, that hateful language, again.

I had not remembered writing to her. I assume now that my mother must have instructed me to sit down and do a drawing or write a letter to

Granny. I seemed to be so real to her then, when I was about seven years old, and yet I had no memory of her at all. But, of course, we had lived with her from the time of my birth until we left Germany. Hers would have been one of the first voices I heard, and her smell would have been as familiar as those of my parents.

She never made it to see us again. The visa for entry to Britain arrived on the day she died. I was bewildered to see my mother with a piece of paper in her hand, suddenly sit down, and sink her head into her lap. My father put his hand on her shoulder, and seeing my surprise, explained that the telegram said that Granny was dead. I don't remember any sound coming from my mother and perhaps I was sent out of the room. That is all the grief I saw. Many years later, when I had visited Grandmother's grave in Switzerland and told my father, he responded by saying, angrily, that he only took my mother there once. As it had upset her, and she had come out crying he would not allow another visit.

The historical hoard of letters I had inherited was fascinating and problematic. I felt it carried a duty for me to do something with it. But each time I went into it, picked up a paper and started reading, the peculiar smell of the paper would trigger an awful feeling, that I called depression. Anyway, I would quickly put the letters away again. Meanwhile, those written in German, especially those in Gothic script, were undecipherable for me. When I had entered secondary school and was assigned to a class that would study German, my parents had me hastily removed and put into the French stream. I realise now that at no time did they help or encourage me to read or write German. They said it was unnecessary. I had thought my ignorance was due to my own laziness. Now I think that I picked up unconsciously on their need to block me from using German as part of my life outside the family.

Then, one day, I was contacted and received a visit from a young Jewish woman from Berlin who was researching pre-war Jewish life in the Prenzlauerberg district of Berlin for an exhibition and a book. A substantial part of this would be about my grandparents, and she was eager for any material I could offer her. At last, I had an external motivator to help me overcome the pain in the papers. Gradually I ironed and filed them in date order and added historical documents as illustration. And this exercise led eventually to me being invited to the unveiling.

As I flew out of Berlin after the unveiling, I began to realise, perhaps for the first time, just how much I had lost. If the Nazi era could have been prevented, I would have grown up in the affectionate circle of a large, extended family, well-rooted in German society and culture and also comfortable in its Jewish identity. My parents would have had the support of their families and been able to go on enjoying the friends of their youth. And I would have been educated in a consistent and positive way, without all the ambivalence and confusion. I would have been free to laugh and cry.

CHAPTER EIGHT

Once upon … a silence

Giselle China

This chapter is a memoir and within it an attempt at exploring the significance of silence in relationship to my understanding of identity and belonging. I am exploring identity not by colour, creed, class, and culture. I am basing it on politics and history. It represents my personal and lived history in the aftermath of growing up in post-war Germany, what I brought to that experience and how it resides in me. This chapter's origins go back some fifteen years to a talk delivered at the MLPC, where I broke the silence.

Starting a journey, both external and internal

I was born in 1944 in the Rhineland region of Germany, at the end of the historical period that ended one perception of the country of my birth and replaced it with another. The word Germany after the war carried a historical burden, a stigma, a label. A stigma is deeply discrediting, as is a label. It disregards the attitudes and the behaviour of the individual. It affirms the "goodness" of others, thereby keeping them emotionally safe. A label was automatically attached to me as German, not Giselle or Giselle China, but what about Gisela? It was England that conferred that name onto me. And I owned it. Could it have been an avoidance of the German name by myself and others and therefore of confronting my Germanness? To speak with Juliet in Shakespeare's *Romeo and Juliet*:

> What's in a name? That which we call a rose
> By any other word would smell as sweet …
> (Act 2, scene 1, lines 90–91)

Or would it?

I was a war baby with the attendant unconscious experiences of a baby, absorbed through the mother and a war-torn environment. My parents had met and married during the war, shortly before my father completed his medical studies, and as an army doctor he was sent to the eastern front advancing towards Stalingrad. My mother was evacuated to the countryside because her house in Cologne had been bombed. She was far from family and friends, pregnant and frightened. I did not meet my father until I was eighteen months old.

Post-war Germans, of necessity, focused intently on their recovery. It was a time of rebuilding with fierce determination and industry, leading towards what would become known as the "German Miracle". Over the years the focus seemed to be on material achievements, the measurable, the phoenix rising from the ashes. At the same time many Germans worked relentlessly at eliminating memories. Could this have been a defence against confronting how they were viewed in the world or by themselves? A hiding behind doing?

My father built his medical practice with my mother's support. Growing up, I did not see much of him as he was working hard. One of my early memories is of a wrecked tank and craters outside my home in the square of the village where my father had settled as a GP. We played there as children, not consciously knowing its significance, maybe subliminally? One day the tank was gone; it became known only by its absence, shrouded in a blanket of silence. The tank for me became a symbol for all that was not talked about, not taught, not explored at school or anywhere else. One day it was there, then it was gone. If the war was spoken about, it was only in fragments and vignettes; these stories invited fantasies. Fragments of history as told by parents, grandparents, aunts, uncles, friends, were endlessly repeated, but never elaborated upon. Nobody sat down with children and told the real story, the history of the war. Their stories could be safely told. Questions seemed to be implicitly discouraged. Now I think of it as the horror that dared not speak its name. It is this silence which the German second-generation child shares with many second-generation survivors of the Holocaust, silence on both sides.

My childhood was also shaped by the beautiful German landscape, music, art, literature, laughter, an all-round education, hospitality, and baking (a tradition which I still cherish). In the context of these contrasting lived experiences, it is important to know one's history is meaningful; it shapes ancestral fate and sensibilities, and it belongs to and shapes one's life. How much more important, then, is it to know one's unspeakable history

The beginning of my inner journey

My first stirrings of political and historical consciousness emerged in my early teens. For a long time I felt vulnerable exploring and thus exposing a past that I had not known and therefore not talked about, either in the Germany I left or as a German in England. It felt like thinking the unthinkable, having left a country that did not speak the unspeakable. Germany continued its cultural traditions as it had always done; comfortable, cosy, warm patterns of welcoming living. What about unwelcome feelings and thoughts? Where were they? Where are they today? I tried, unconsciously, to escape my story, but it caught me eventually. The impossibility of surrendering memories, known, sensed, or unthought, made it hard to take root completely in another country and, as I was starting to realise, in another language. For a long time, buried deeply in the recesses of my mind, lurked the question, "Do I, as a German war child, have a right to go to this dark place?" While this thinking was irrational, it remained persistent. I felt contaminated by my country's history, I felt a victim to it, innocent, but blemished. I dared not speak of it, for I believed that only the innocent victims had that right. For many years it had seemed a Jewish prerogative to speak, to be called "second-generation". A split approach to the same trauma. Feelings are not the prerogative of the survivors of the Holocaust and their descendants. They belong to us all from the second generation and all of us as human beings in an uncertain world; pain does not discriminate. I felt haunted by the half-glimpsed truth of that trauma. So, like it or not, I had to confront the reality of the two "second generations", seemingly speaking two different languages. Eventually I was forced to give emotional attention to my history and how it relates to the present. Distance does not dupe memory … I had to embark on this journey.

In my Germany the past is always present, no one provokes it. I emigrated to England in 1970 with a sense of leaving the past behind, and after arriving realised it was still present in me. I was attracted to England, first as a school girl, later as a university student. I fell in love with an Englishman who is half French, and we married shortly after my graduation. Here my children were born. We settled in North London where many German Jewish refugees lived at that time. I felt both shy of them and attracted to them and sought to listen to them speaking German in the local parks and shops. I did not know that I might have been homesick for the Germany I had wanted to leave so much.

Silence and a dream of elsewhere

Arriving in England I did not speak German, I was silent in German. With one exception: sometimes I spoke to my young son in German. He silenced me by telling me not to "talk that" and later "talk properly". Speaking German in England has never felt comfortable. It seems to have been one of the second-generation legacies to disavow German. I had no German connections here, nor did I seek any. I did not attend any German functions. I taught German and French at an English grammar school; it never occurred to me to teach at a German school. When I happened to encounter anybody German we spoke in English. This silence was not a silence imposed on me. I conspired and colluded with it. The silence also kept me safe from being known as German. I hid behind the mask of another language. This hiding place took me back to the dream of my adolescence, the dream of an elsewhere, a yonder.

My family background is European, of which the most significant aspect for me was my grandmother being French. I was extraordinarily proud of her as she was so different to the world around me; petite, elegant, vivacious, quietly strong in a charming way, speaking German with a pronounced French accent. She displayed none of the then familiar

German desire for conformity, the conformity that stifled both creativity and emotions. She seemed exotic. I adored her. I did not recognise the fact that she did not speak French with us; could this have been for political reasons? Both her Frenchness and the concept of Europe were to play a significant role in my unconscious and later conscious life that shaped me. I longed to go outside: outside the Germany I knew to be culturally enriching and emotionally secretive. I longed for her Frenchness to also be mine. I turned it into the reverie that ascribed to Frenchness or the dream of it, the magical powers to enchant and transform. I imagined a bigger, less stifling world. This fantasy incorporated an existential concept: unconsciously I broadened out my unnamed horror into a hopeful future. The German child knew without knowing that the world needs to be embraced, connected, linked. Isolation misses the point of sharing and hope, namely to make strength out of fragility. My utopian dream represented my first intimation of feeling divided and wanting to break away; an internal process projected onto an outside place, a place of both fantasy and reality in silence.

Silence and identity

My arrival in England was like entering a metaphorical white room, culturally unfurnished, academically well explored, yet to be filled with life and colours and hopefully leading to a sense of home. I spoke the language fluently, yet had no experienced knowledge of the underlying, unspoken culture which informs every language. In that white room there was no one with whom to share what I call the "do you remember when ...?" moments. Or even more significantly, the wordlessly known experiences of joint childhood history, kindergarten, schools, songs, customs, and games. What was I to make of the white room, a room without personal history? Would I graft a new identity onto my German one, would these identities clash, contradict, eliminate parts of me? Or would they fuse, integrate the new with the old, assimilate, or could the whole become bigger than the sum of its parts? There are many ways of conceiving our identities, our lives, of shaping memories and narratives; identities are malleable and multifaceted.

The England of 1970 seemed to know itself with confidence. It represented a different world then, not only different to my country, but also very different to the England of today. It was an England with a strong identity, and was less culturally diverse. This sense of identity and the British pride in itself were in stark contrast to anything I had known of national pride. I secretly envied that sense of belonging with such seeming certainty, without fear or shame. I came here as an outsider who also represented the enemy; politically I was fearful and ashamed.

Identity and voice

My perception of the country of my birth, my fatherland, was split. It is my personal perception and led to the exploration of my two countries and the languages within. What was the impact on my sense of identity and belonging? Or should I say identities?

This split manifested itself powerfully when I first attempted to integrate the disparate parts of my journey of exploration, particularly the thinking and the feeling. Initially it was informed by the experience of my childhood, namely to implicitly ask no questions, resulting in silence. But each aspect of my story was beginning to clamour for a voice of equal importance: immigration, silence, historical facts, personal history, shame, guilt, courage, language in which to speak and languages that carry emotions. I was both frightened and excited to experience in that moment the possibility of the present relating to the past. I hesitated to speak my German emotional voice, and yet, like anybody released from the tethers of silence, I not only wanted to speak, I had to speak. I also realised that I had needed to find another language in which to break the silence. As a second-generation German I had found my English voice. It is the English voice and not the voice in English which allowed me to speak. The journey had been long. Another question arose: had I castrated my Germanness or fertilised it elsewhere? Or had the English voice allowed for an opening to return to my mother tongue?

I needed to paint the emotional background of my Germanness from a place of new belonging, before I could return to the beginning and its shadow. I also needed to acknowledge to myself that I was not speaking of my personal silence and my personal secret alone: I was also addressing the collective, the German one. In that place I felt no longer isolated. I was breaking the silence and revealing the secret of me, the German woman who was born into a specific period of history. I was also looking at my different experiences of being German, not just one overwhelming aspect that imposed the dreadful silence of the long shadows. The second-generation German is afflicted and affected by silence and secrets. I continued to explore how silence shapes identity, how it shaped *my* identity. I was beginning to find the voice that could explore the truth of how history affected me and carried me off to a shore of new beginning. I also acknowledged that people are not nations. Did my relationship to my nation necessitate the journey?

Identity and language

Through telling my story I started to make sense of the silence that tainted my identity, whilst asking questions. Is it history I am looking at, or myself in relation to my history? Do stories contain a universal truth outside the personal? Does my story contain a universal truth faced by many immigrants? A narrative uses logic and reason to reconstruct an experience. Superficially, it helps maintain one's known sense of self; underneath lurks the subversive voice of uncertainty and familiar fear of change. Or in my case, a longing for change: to break the silence. Speaking requires both a language and language to speak. I had disowned German as the language of my "departure". I had to reach for the language of my "arrival". Could I find the language with which to speak of which I knew not what? I knew something of the character of the object, my country's history that had affected me, but I had not thought it. That, which Bollas (1987) calls "the unthought known". Making the thought known helped me find the courage to tell the story, to speak the past in a country in which the story did not take place.

Where there is an "unthought known" the imagination works to finish the stories we tell ourselves and others. So how could I speak? Which language did I speak? Even more importantly, which language spoke me? Or could this question be taken even further? Was there a dialogue of languages; which language spoke what? Which language belonged to me and to which language did I belong? Was my new country a disguise? Or a new identity? Or was it like the emperor's new clothes? Again, Bollas (1979) comes to my aid. His thinking helped me define my new country as my transformational object. Was I grafting a new identity onto my German one? Identity is about relationships, it does not exist in a void.

Identity is mirroring, being in context and being reflected back. In my country of origin no reflection existed, the mirror was covered.

Feeling accepted and wanted creates a sense of belonging that allows identity to safely unfold. Identity requires security and trust. Secrecy endangers a secure sense of identity. Growing up with a sense of the unspoken, or even worse, the unspeakable, created an identity that doubted itself. What about the fact that an emigrant becomes an outsider? How does that affect a sense of identity? An immigrant is an outsider. Does an immigrant remain an outsider? Was I speaking as a vulnerable outsider? To speak or not to speak? Of difference or indifference? The relentlessness of needing to speak turned into a drumbeat of determination, emphatic and relentless. There are other nationals in the world with the same questions and conflict. I thought I was alone.

My languages

As a child I lost, or maybe found, myself in books and music, a place where intellect and emotions met safely. I played instruments and made music alone and with others.

At university I read English, French, and philosophy. I felt at home with intellectual pursuits and with the thinking of feeling, as opposed to feeling the feelings. I indulged in the love of languages, the otherness that I was craving. English became my language of life, Eros, as opposed to my mother tongue, Thanatos, the death instinct. My emotional language is my second language, not my mother tongue. There was no translation, not for me. I felt reborn in a new language. French was my language of dreaming, onto which I projected the *grand-mère*, the idealised mother/grandmother of my emotional search. Music is my safe language with great significance in my life and impact on my immigration. It is a language both wordless and emotional. The understanding of music has also informed my understanding of yet another language, that of psychoanalysis. What happens when the intonation is off, either slightly and therefore difficult to identify, or noticeably so? It can create tension. A tension can be resolved when identified and adjusted. Or it can create a split. Music and analysis for me have much in common: they touch the emotions, they are about tensions, about dissonance and transformation, about joyless cadences with equal endless repetitions or repetition compulsion, about making sense, about dissonance seeking resolution and leading to consonance. Music is my language of the heart and the language that I did not need to abandon. Most importantly, it required no translation. It lived. Music represents the wordless communication of both mind and emotion, and not in silence.

I see music as a journey, a metaphor, where there are themes that are introduced, developed, and elaborated upon and brought to a conclusion; where there are dialogues, relationships of the themes; they are played out against and with each other, in major and in minor keys. However, it is not the music that carries the emotion: the listener attaches his or her emotional response to the sound. This then gives it meaning, just like the reader of this chapter will give it meaning.

The wound of silence

The child and young person who speaks in this text did not know that a secret is like a wound. I was born into a secret; today I call it the wound of silence. I had no concept of its meaning or its effect. The conspiracy allowed the feelings of shame and guilt to fester in the darkness of silence. In Germany, post 1945, despite or maybe because of the remarkable social, political, and economic achievements, awareness of the horrors committed remained an open wound of historic, if not personal, culpability. In my experience German eyes were averted from this wound, silence reigned. But just as in music, silence speaks. It is like holding one's breath or taking a breath. Eros or Thanatos, life or death?

Eva Hoffman (2004) eloquently describes how she dealt with her parents' silent pain simply by not addressing it.

> The Germans were the demonic force in the universe, and the duty to abhor them was almost as strong and morally tinctured as the obligation to respect those on whom their cruelty was inflicted. In addition, those closest to the events, post war children, or Hitler's children, have the least knowledge of all. Their families lived their history, future generations learnt about it. Post war children lived the profound effect without knowing it. (p. 14)

Just as Eva Hoffman writes from the Jewish perspective, so Wolfgang Koeppen (2004) speaks from the German side. Koeppen, one of the great twentieth-century German writers, for a time lost the words to speak. When he spoke again he discovered and wrote about the preferred form for German literature at that time:

> a clean slate with … only the markings of a very few on it— the ones with cast iron alibis. It was a very German solution— Schwamm darueber! [Let's forget it!]—unjust and evasive and superficial, an extension of collective amnesia. (p. vii)

Koeppen was not prepared to write on a clean slate. He remembered and criticised and was savaged: he was shown hostility, revulsion, and repugnance. He was continuously told, "Let's look on the bright side." Koeppen stopped writing literature and "emigrated" into the writing of travel stories.

Silence broken—words spoken

Which words needed to be spoken that avoided them becoming travel stories? Professing horror and outrage is the illusion of a journey. I could not even feel outrage. All I felt was shame. I had not been able to speak of that shame, instead I mourned. Starting off life, lacking a sense of safety and security, represents archetypal mourning. Freud (1917e) tells us that mourning is "regularly the reaction to … loss, of some abstraction, a country, a liberty, an ideal …" (p. 237). He links mourning to melancholia: "The distinguishing mental features of melancholia are a lowering of the self-regarding feelings to a degree that finds utterance in self-reproaches" (p. 237). The melancholia that Freud describes links shame and mourning to guilt. Disenfranchised grief involves feeling sorrow, fear, uncertainty, and worry about being heard, understood, respected, severely judged, or rejected.

I had internalised my German shame and guilt to such an extent that I scrutinised the world around me for any projections onto anything or anyone German, the German stigma, hopefully not me as a person. Shame does not easily find a voice. Was I ashamed of my country? Did

I dare ask, truly ask: "And what did *you* do in the war?" Could I trust? Could I trust anybody? Could anybody trust? I could not think of their suffering. I thought with the narcissism of the child. I encountered passive/aggressive attacks on my entitlement to those feelings, as if there was a competition about pain. How can suffering be measured? When I arrived in England children were still playing at being soldiers with Germans being the "baddies". The same went for the perception of the German language as expressing something dark; the German villain resides, to some extent, in the conscious and unconscious use of it in films and literature. The early James Bond films serve as an example, with the attendant use of the harsh, concise, mocked German accent.

The sound of German can be poetic, soft and musical, rhythmic and melodic, yet the intonation in the spoken everyday language can be perceived as hard and harsh. While my English has been fluent in vocabulary, grammar, and style, for many years I was sometimes misunderstood in my intentions when I became passionate about a subject, a thought, an exploration. I was accused of being aggressive and therefore controlling, labelled through my intonation, my German intonation, which was frequently an intonation of emotion. Feeling misunderstood catapulted me back to my emotional childhood where, by thinking differently, both dreamily and emotionally, I had learnt to automatically assume that I had done something wrong without understanding the wrong. It was my first therapist who helped me understand the aspects and nuances of difference. Incidentally, two of my three therapists were immigrants: South African, a German who had fled Germany as a child, and a British Jewish analyst. The "otherness" was most openly acknowledged with my South African therapist. I never spoke German to or with my German-born therapist. And the "Jewish question" was studiously avoided with my Jewish analyst. However, when the Jewish question is addressed, the speaking binds us, as my story within my story demonstrates so simply and powerfully.

In the 1970s I became friends with my neighbours who were German refugees. They felt like loving, surrogate grandparents. She came from a distinguished Berlin family who had managed to escape; her husband had lost his entire family in the Holocaust. One day he stood up, he looked very serious. He wondered whether he could ask me a question, I nodded. These, his words, touched me deeply: "When I left Germany I swore that I would never kiss a German woman again. Please may I kiss you?" The importance of breaking silence in the basic human encounter can bring profound and healing change to both parties. In this chapter I am passing on this kiss. It addresses the secret that is so powerfully described in the poem "The Secret Sits" by Robert Frost (1942):

> We dance round in a ring and suppose,
> But the secret sits in the middle and knows. (p. 71)

I stopped dancing, I started writing, and discovered that writing does not equal speaking. The silence remained, the identity veiled: linked to speaking a language is the importance and meaning of accents. Many years ago I was struck deeply by hearing someone say: "Just because I speak with an accent does not mean that I think with an accent." An accent denotes other, difference, difference of emotional and cultural thinking and perceptions. An accent alerts the listener and is perceived as defining the speaker. It may include prejudice from the outset. When can difference become an exciting opportunity for growth? I do not speak with an accent, or so I am told. Some people detect an accent and feel the need to apologise, implying that the accent defines me, setting me apart as other. It sets me into a context that for each listener will be different, that creates a transference onto me. We are in a different place from where we started, separate, different as well as unified in the otherness. Others say that nobody would know that I was German. What does that say about them and me? Is not having a discernible accent another form of hiding? Is not having an accent a defence against the effects of otherness, of being an outsider?

Speaking a language fluently and with an almost imperceptible accent is misleading in its assumption that a language spoken corresponds with a culture known and understood. This is compounded by my not asking questions for a long time. I was forever on the alert to decode what was not yet known, probably an excellent preparation for my psychoanalytic work, a creative sublimation arising from something initially deeply disturbing. I chose a profession that requires exploration, hopefully leading to understanding. My understanding of my musical language gives me the guidance to know when to hold back questions, when to be judicious, but not forbidden to ask questions. It had escaped me for a long time that I had chosen a profession the tools of which are language and words; and the use of self, the self that depends on a secure sense of identity to be effective. For a time I was still speaking on behalf of another, the patient, until I started to speak of me.

Becoming a therapist in another country and another language, away from the missing emotion of my mother tongue, gave me permission to explore feelings, language, meaning, facts, and memories in order to facilitate communication. To ask questions. My daughter at the age of eight or nine informed me that I was a therapist because I was so nosy. She had not meant it kindly. I had not understood what her accusation later helped me to understand. She had given me the gift of knowing that curiosity turns towards the potential of truth. My historical experience was that of living avoidance. English, as opposed to German, formulates questions much less directly or confrontationally. It assumes a cultural reticence, which allowed me to be reticent, too.

Speaking freely

My psychic survival was made possible by the dream of otherness, a childlike dream and a concept—I called it Europe—that was bigger than the sum of its parts. It was first ensured by my escape into words and the language of music. It manifested itself in leaving my country and arriving in another land, and in doing that, giving birth to an emotional language that allowed me to return. Finally, remembering my German meant putting together the pieces of the present and the past in my existential place in the world, one that is encompassing.

By leaving I had attempted, unconsciously, to escape the conspiracy of silence. I took flight and yet I am not a refugee. I, along with many other "second generations", seem to have absorbed the feelings of the times, rather than the context which gave rise to them. A theme of shadows. There is in me a shadow, the darkest shadow of all, namely the thought that if I had been an adult during those times, of what would I have been capable? Facing the shadow side in us all is terrifying. Emerging from the silence evokes feelings of profound sadness and an acknowledgement that the evil perpetrated by the German nation is a potential of humanity, wherever in the world, and therefore also of me. A potential from which it is impossible to escape.

My lack of courage to speak has been painful to recognise and hard to bear. Not speaking trapped me, speaking felt liberating. It finally made sense of one aspect of my feelings of guilt: I had done nothing wrong. However, I had failed to do something, I had failed to speak, to address what was a crippling mask. To lift the German mask seems to have taken much longer to do for second-generation Germans who chose to live abroad. Germans living in Germany seem to have started on that quest sooner. Bernhard Schlink (1997) risked breaking the silence from within Germany. I, in a diaspora, did not catch up so fast. Or maybe exile and the place allocated to the German perception did not allow it.

My past was shaped by silence, by varying kinds of silence; silence that is also known in the consulting room. The silence of guilt and shame, of mourning: the emotional silence. That which I chose to call the wound of silence. There was the personal silence, theirs and mine, the collective silence, and the conspiracy of silence. And, just like in music, or in the consulting room, silence speaks. It is filled with what had been said or omitted. For me it became the reality of a gap that needed to be filled by finding the voice to speak. Now my identity incorporates that longed-for assimilation; being a foreigner in a country I love, belonging yet different, where my Germanness and my European parentage is embraced, and where I embrace being both English and German, warts and all.

Afterthought

After the London bombing on 7 July 2005, at a time when I was exploring thoughts about the paper on which this chapter is based, London felt like a village. People pulled together as Londoners. I felt like a Londoner, a foreign Londoner, but a Londoner nonetheless. My London had been attacked. I realised then in my deepest being that I was home, that London is home. The multicultural aspect of London became apparent to all. This had not existed in the 1970s. Suddenly it did not matter that I was German. But that was easy; this time I was on the side of the innocent, not on the side of the evil of terrorism. People were busy fearing all Muslims as the perpetrators. Again, fear informs blaming the other, the not us.

Immigration is complex and multifaceted. There is no single threat. There are simply stories with rich and varied issues, some of which belong to me, the German alone, and some are part of the immigrants' experience, the immigrants who are also citizens of the world. It is at this point that I am reminded of the impact John F. Kennedy had on Germany and me when, upon giving a speech in Berlin in 1963, he ended with the words: "*Ich bin ein Berliner.*" Today I am a Londoner. I am home as well as knowing from where I came, knowing this place for the first time.

References

Bollas, C. (1979). The transformational object. *International Journal of Psychoanalysis*, *60*(1): 97–107.

Bollas, C. (1987). *The Shadow of the Object: Psychoanalysis of the Unthought Known.* New York: Columbia University Press.

Hoffman, E. (2004). *After Such Knowledge.* London: Secker & Warburg.

Freud, S. (1917e). Mourning and melancholia. *S. E.*, *14*: 237–258. London: Hogarth.

Frost, R. (1942). *A Witness Tree.* New York: Henry Holt.

Koeppen, W. (2004). *Death in Rome.* London: Granta.

Schlink, B. (1997). *The Reader.* London: Phoenix House.

Shakespeare, W. (1675). *Romeo and Juliet.* W. J. Craig (Ed.). *The Complete Works of William Shakespeare.* London: Oxford University Press, 1914.

CHAPTER NINE

The challenge of "home"

Shula Wilson

Fairy Tale

He built himself a house,
    his foundations,
    his stones,
    his walls,
    his roof over head,
    his chimney and smoke his view from the window.
He made himself a garden,
    his fence,
    his thyme,
    his earthworm,
    his evening dew,
He cut out his bit of sky above.
And he wrapped the garden in the sky
and the house in the garden
and packed the lot in a handkerchief
and went off
lone as an arctic fox
through the cold

unending

rain

into the world.

Miroslav Holub

(Heaney & Hughes, 2005)

Holub called his poem "a fairy tale" which suggests that the home has an inner dwelling, it is not just the outside protective shell. It is a dream, a wish, and at the same time also a necessary provision for being and surviving in the world. The poem describes the creation of a comforting and protecting inner home; a home whether real or imaginary has to be bounded by walls, roof, and a fence.

Holub creates a tension between the dream world of "Fairy Tale" and the reality of walls and garden fence, suggesting that it is necessary to have a notion of home even when it is in a fantasy form, such as a fairy tale. Having an "internal home" provides the sense of security and strength needed to survive "the cold unending rain".

In the less poetic words of Bollnow: "Home is the means by which man carves out of the universal space a special and to some extent private space and thus separates inner space from outer space" (1961, p. 33).

Most of us would associate "home" with positive notions such as: "safety", "comfort", or "warmth". However, a dysfunctional home may betray the trust invested in it and become dangerous and threatening. To examine the complexity of the notion of "home", I will first reflect on my own experiences and memories. Then I will follow Jim's journey from his broken home that was loaded with dread and fear, to finding the external and internal place where he could "feel at home". How he struggled to survive despite the haunting childhood memories of danger and neglect, which impaired and distorted his ability to create and maintain both outer and inner home.

My home

When a colleague asked me, "Are you going home this summer?" I was confused. What does she mean? She seems to think that London is not my home and in her mind I belong elsewhere. Is it perhaps because I did not grow up in England and English is not my mother tongue? This took me back to the times when my father was telling me stories about his childhood in Romania. In his memoirs my father writes:

> Since I remember myself Ileana was our helper, she was a Romanian girl from a remote village. She worked in our house for many years and spoke good Yiddish. With me she only spoke Yiddish. When she had time, we would play and sometimes we went for walks. I liked her very much. One day, I was not yet 4, she was very happy and told me that she was given a week's holiday and that she is going home. I was a bit confused and went to my mother to ask: "What is Ileana talking about? What is her home?" My mother told me that Ileana is going to the village where her parents live and she will stay there for a week. I was confused and asked mother: "And where is my home?" My mother answered: "Your home is in the land of Israel." (Wagner, 2000, p. 77)

Like the child who became my father, I am still asking: "Do I have a home?" and then: "Where is home, what is a home." This is the beginning of a long journey searching for some understanding of this mundane yet elusive concept: *home*.

In Hebrew, my first language, the entry for home occupies a large space in the dictionary. Most of those entries had been created about a hundred years ago, when the dormant Hebrew had been revived from a scholar's language that for 2,000 years had been used mainly for religious purposes, into a modern everyday language. Establishing a common language was a very significant element in creating a homeland for the Jews. Many new words had to be invented in the process of adjusting an ancient tongue, to express current reality. Combinations of the word "home" with another noun were used to describe institutions that were not mentioned in the old Hebrew script. For example, the translation of "school" is "home of the book"; "hospital", "home of the sick"; "prison", "home of jail"; "factory", "home of manufacture", and so on. Perhaps this was one way the wandering Jews were trying to express a wish for a permanent place of being—a home.

My mother's mother tongue was German. This was the language I heard her speaking to her mother, her sisters, and other relatives from "there". Yet I don't remember my mother trying to include me, to introduce me to her mother's tongue. Perhaps it was an attempt at preventing German, the language of her past, from contaminating me. She often spoke to my father in German, but although he was fluent, he always answered her in Hebrew. Growing up in Israel in the 1950s created a conflict in relation to German. It was the language of those who wanted to destroy us, yet for my mother it was also the language of culture and progress. Perhaps I, as a rebellious child, did not want anything to do with it. But it was all around me. My first language is Hebrew, I love speaking Hebrew, but intimacy is rarely there. My fantasy is that by keeping me out of the German language, I was denied the intimacy it could have afforded. At the same time as blocking the lingual link with my mother's past, it freed me from feeling part of the middle-European enclave that my parents came from and were part of, and allowed me to integrate and become part of the newly formed homeland.

I wanted to believe that I belonged to the "new brave generation" free of the diaspora burden. We spoke an ancient yet new language, not contaminated by the shameful association of weakness, of people who (so we thought) were taken "like lambs to the slaughter". We saw ourselves as being strong, protecting and defending our country, and turning the desert into blooming gardens. At school we did "agriculture", working the little vegetable plot in the yard. In the youth movement—away from our parents' world—we were preparing ourselves to build a strong, just country. But still, something was missing; I did not know what.

Ideas of home

Papadopoulos (2002) suggests that home is both the perceived place of origin as well as the desired destination, the end, the aim: where we are coming from and where we want to be. We can also see home as the transitional object that facilitates our efforts to adjust to life out of the womb, by offering comfort and reassurance. It represents both the wish to be held and the need to breathe freely.

The notion of home, which is what most of us take for granted, is how we unconsciously read life and fulfil our desires. For many people a home country is where one is expected to feel part of the collective, which also provides cultural identity. Leaving the home country could be regarded as a betrayal and the defector should be punished; though sometimes one does not need to leave the home country to feel punished and betrayed by one's own home. As we will see in Jim's story, people who feel unwanted and uncared for may feel betrayed and punished, yet they often don't know why and what they have done to deserve it.

Our first home, the place where we are introduced to the world, creates the blueprint and gives us a reference point and angle that will influence how we will conceptualise the world and our place in it, especially in relation to familiarity and intimacy. Mother tongue, the language of our first home, should become the inner dwelling of intimacy and familiarity.

The French philosopher Merleau-Ponty (1962) discusses the tension between the concept of the perfect body held in the mind which is the "wished for body" as opposed to the "the body in the moment", which is the body we actually possess, with all its imperfections. Taking the liberty to paraphrase Merleau-Ponty and exchange "body" for "home" could provide us with a clear illustration of the tension between the "wished for home" and "the home in the moment". Most people who left their home of origin, in particular immigrants, are holding a parallel view of home: the home they inhabit wherever they are "in the moment", and a "back home" concept, to describe and relate to where they had been and left behind. The concept of "back home" is used to compare the current reality with the memories of what had become the inner home. What is inner home? What is it made of and how do we use it?

Jim's story

Jim's story is an example of what can happen when home is unreliable and threatening, when one needs to seek refuge from a dangerous home. There are many ways in which people may feel excluded or deprived of what should have been their home. What comes to mind are refugees, those who are forced to leave their home. However, most refugees are still able to hold on to the positive and comforting memory of home and carry it with them, like in Holub's "Fairy Tale" poem. Not so for Jim. His story which unfolds in the next few pages is about the struggle to survive when the blueprint of home is marred with uncertainty, fear, and rejection; how distorted the inner home can become, so it turns into a dreadful threat with no safe place.

Jim came to me after a phone call from his daughter asking if I could help her father. "He is depressed," she said. "The GP prescribed antide-pressants which seems to have triggered frequent hallucinations and very morbid thoughts. He says he wants to die. I am so worried about him."

When Jim came to see me, he talked about his "panic attacks" which he described as severe trembling and uncontrolled shaking, weeping, and unexplained haunting fears. The most disturbing symptom was the fear to stay inside his own home. Jim and his wife had moved to their new house about a year prior to commencing therapy. They wanted to improve their living conditions and to be near his two adult children and their families. But somehow it did not work. Jim could not bear staying in the new house after sunset. He felt engulfed by hostility.

When I first met Jim, he was spending most of his free time at his daughter's home. He saw his inability to stay in his own house as his fault and a weakness, which fed into the anxiety caused by the fear that the house provoked. Jim appears as a solid, polite, and well-presented per-son who is able to articulate his thoughts in a clear and fluent manner. He is the youngest of five children, his nearest siblings are twin brothers who were very close to each other, and little Jim felt alone and isolated.

The therapeutic relationship

At this point I need to make a confession: the service that Jim was seek-ing therapy from is designated for people who are affected by disabil-ity. Jim did not have any physical or other recognised disability. Strictly speaking, I should not have accepted him for therapy. How come I found myself bending the rules for him? On reflection it may have been that I could not bring myself to add another rejection to a list that was already too long. However, I also believe that by breaking the rule, I was responding to his need to be special, to have someone stepping out of line for him, to be given a shelter against the odds. Also, the uncertainty embedded in his fragile sense of belonging echoed strongly with my own feeling of being an outsider.

He was a survivor who used to look after himself and others. I respected him for it. Once I realised boundaries had been broken it heightened my awareness of my subjective attitude and the necessary vigilance in monitoring how this may affect our therapeutic relationship. Jim was consumed by fear. What made it unbearable for him was his inability to make any sense of it. He was terrified but did not know what he was afraid of. A metaphor he used to describe his experience was: "It is like when a computer goes all wrong, it just makes horrible noises and buzzes and fusses, and whatever knob you press, just makes it worse, it is being completely out of control, not being able to stop what is happening to you." I felt as confused and unable to make sense of this as Jim was.

Jim recalled his early memories, of him and his brothers hiding under the kitchen table while his father beat his mother and threatened to kill her and the children.

They lived in a poor and crowded neighbourhood where everyone knew each other, and the care of children was shared. So, when Jim managed to escape from his father, he would invariably find an open door nearby to hide behind, and if he was lucky, to be offered some food and warmth. Then came World War II. Father went away and Jim and his siblings were evacuated to the country. The countryside was so different from anything he knew: the open green spaces, the fresh air, the birds and the animals. It was all new and made him happy, but he was not sure how to be with the village children. They did not welcome him, rarely included him in their games. He felt lonely and confused. During the two years they stayed in the village, mother came only once, to tell them that their father had been killed in action. Did little Jim think his father was killed because he wished him dead?

Two months into therapy Jim was talking about his feeling of dread and anger when hearing or reading the news. He said that he is really worried about the young children who are being abused and sometimes disappear without trace. I was still puzzled: what is the connection? The next session, Jim started by talking about the war:

> "During the war, after we came back from the 'country', we had to live in the underground tunnels because of the Blitz. My mother was a warden, she was making sure everything was right in our part of the tunnel. One evening I was out playing with some other kids, when a man came and asked me to show him where the

telephone booth is. I did not think much of it and went along to show him, and after a few steps he grabbed and pushed me into the bushes. He was trying to do things to me. I did not understand what he was trying to do, but I knew it was not right. I was terrified but somehow I managed to escape and run back to our part of the tunnel. My mother did not notice at all that I was missing, she was much too busy looking after other people for her to pay any attention to me." He paused, took a deep breath, and then said: "I could have been dead, and nobody would have known. I never talked about it before, I never told anybody."

For more than fifty years Jim had been carrying alone the painful wounds caused by the fear and the shame of the abuse and the neglect.

Winnicott (1986) said that there is a big proportion of all people who successfully hide a need for a breakdown; the potential breakdown is awaiting an outside trigger. Perhaps Jim's panic attacks could be seen as Winnicott's "breakdown". What was the trigger, and how does it link to the current fear of being in his own home? The experience of the assault at the age of eight was a traumatic event. It was an experience that Jim could not digest and absorb and therefore remained in his psyche as a "foreign body". Laplanche and Pontalis (1988) suggested that the outcome of the trauma is the incapacity of the psychical apparatus to illuminate the disturbing affect and to keep balance.

After the war, as Jim was growing up, he tried to forget the past and start afresh. Jim managed to suppress his bad memories and never talked about his childhood. He was busy, finishing his education, finding work, marrying the girl he loved, and looking after his young family. He was doing well and did not want to let the disturbing childhood memories interfere with his life. He was able, for a time, to encapsulate the painful thoughts and memories and push them into the very back of his mind. When his first beloved wife died, the capsule holding the past started to leak and his memories started to haunt him.

After a few sad and lonely years, he married his second wife, hoping that having a partner would help him to keep the past at bay. But the new relationship turned out to be difficult and somewhat disappointing. This, combined with ageing, caused the capsule to burst and the raw unbearable childhood memories came back. He was thrown into an inner world where there is no safe place; violence and threats at home, rejection, abuse, and neglect outside. In his mind his current home had become the home he needed to escape from as a child. Nothing was safe anymore; all was contaminated with fear and dread. The home became a symbol of deception; it was supposed to protect but instead there were threats and attacks.

Telling the "secret", exposing the traumatising "foreign body" seems to have been a turning point on several levels. Jim and I survived it; he was not being punished for telling his tale and I was not destroyed or "shocked" into incapacity (although this carries its own disappointment as we will see later). Also, by talking about the assault, the neglect, and the emotions that he had experienced, Jim got in touch with the first "clue" which could lead to an understanding and perhaps find some sense in what felt at the time a very chaotic space. Surviving the test of exposing his story and feeling understood opened up the "flood gate" and enabled Jim to talk freely about what came to his mind. It was a cold winter day when Jim was telling me:

> "When we were in the country as evacuees, I went out with the others to play on the frozen river. I can't remember how it all happened but suddenly I was under the ice in the freezing cold water. I felt trapped, I thought I will die there, I did not think anyone will come to get me out. They did. My sister saw me missing and shouted for help."

This was an important piece of the puzzle, an illustration of Jim's experiencing fear, danger, and feeling abandoned, yet he was remembered and survived. I believe that he also experienced me as remembering him in the therapy and giving him help like his sister did. The existence of an inner part of himself, which can be resilient if remembered or witnessed empathically, was confirmed. We could now see that those life-threatening childhood events could be the cause of his current panic attacks, suggesting that it could be a delayed reaction, that as a child, when he actually experienced frightening events, he could not afford to acknowledge and react to the terror. Admitting weakness would have been too dangerous. As he had neither an external nor an internal safe place to call home, he had to "freeze" his reaction and store it away.

Only now, when he feels more or less secure and his children are not dependent on him anymore, his unconscious "allowed" the frozen reaction to thaw and to come up to the surface. Jim started to realise that he was feeling and reacting to events that took place in his childhood. Being able to make sense seems to reduce the symptoms. Jim was reporting on improvement in his everyday life. He sometimes managed to stay in his house for the night and was able to stand up to his wife. I commented that perhaps what attracted him to his wife could have been the familiarity, as he did find in his wife many characteristics which were similar to how he remembered his mother; a strong personality that often gives a double message. For example, saying: "'This is my lovely baby' to other people and then ignoring me, her very same baby."

You are not listening to me

One of the complaints against his wife was that she does not understand him. It took me a while to realise that he was also talking about me. It was a session after a holiday break and Jim arrived about five minutes late. Jim came late for several weeks prior to that holiday, which was very unlike him. He reported having a panic attack when he was at home and his daughter and her family were there.

"I was in a bad way. I had a fight with my wife. She is not helpful when I am not well. I did tell her I feel scared inside, but she just says, there is nothing to be scared of. ... I need to find a way to understand what it was. I was off my food; my stomach was in knots ..."

Although he was talking about his wife, I could clearly hear his anger directed also at me. What have I done to trigger the images of people who are there to help and support, but actually they are not doing what they are supposed to do? I knew I had disappointed him, but how? And then "the penny dropped". Jim was trying to communicate a message to me through his lateness and I was not responding, I was ignoring him. I was useless, like his mother, and his wife. I did not notice his "action language". When I finally acknowledged that my failing to pay attention to his lateness felt as if I was ignoring and abandoning him, Jim said:

"Maybe, I just want it all to go away, I want to be normal again, I need somebody who will understand me."

I see this session as another breakthrough. Jim's anger was heard and acknowledged, and again, both of us survived it. The expression of anger did not result either in punishment or destruction. This session took place about a year into therapy, and there were no more panic attacks. About three months later Jim moved to a new house, leaving behind the house that made him so fearful and depressed. In his words he is "happy, but not yet a hundred per cent". He is now revisiting his painful memories, but this time from a position of his newly acquired strength:

"I remember running to the tube, I know it is real, but I cannot remember anything after, if somebody would have only asked me where I was, but nobody did" (like me not noticing his lateness).

Jim is now able to own and face the horrors of his past as real events. By doing so, what he tried to push away, as if it was a bad dream, does not haunt him anymore. However, Jim is still not convinced that he is safe, that he is not going to be punished. But now he is able to own his life story, and he is beginning to seek his personal truth by separating fantasy from reality yet acknowledging that they are interrelated.

Jim is talking about "the time when I would not have to come here anymore, when I will feel comfortable in my new house". I believe that Jim's natural resilience and his ability for self-healing are the main contributors to his well-being. My part is mainly due to being aware of him as a "special" client, the special child he had never been.

I believe that my "foreignness", which manifested itself through my accent, facilitated an engagement through a "second language" which afforded a detour and distance from Jim's affect-ridden mother tongue (Smith, 1991). When the mother tongue is overloaded with difficult emotions, the use of a foreign language can bring the ambiguity which enables distance and perspective.

Home is the familiar environment, which includes language, landscape, smells, sounds, people, and memories of early experiences. For those of us who were fortunate to have an overall positive childhood, their inner home (as in the opening "Fairy Tale" poem) will be positively familiar, and in due course will enable them to gather the elements needed to create their own home. For the likes of Jim, their inner home is made of a great deal of pain, mistrust, and fear. When he was a young adult, Jim's youthful energy had carried him forward, while avoiding and suppressing the darkness of his past and the accumulative trauma of his childhood.

Discussion

Looking again at Jim's experience brings thoughts of nomads and the plasticity of home. Even as a child, Jim knew that something was badly wrong at his home. He grew up in a close community, where he came across fathers who were kind and mothers who were attentive and caring. So why was his home so different? Little Jim needed a reason that would explain and make sense of his dysfunctional world. In order to maintain some control in his chaotic and frightening reality, his omnipotent fantasy led him to assume responsibility. He started to believe that all that is happening is because of him. When his father died in the war, he felt as if his wish had come true, and his deep sense of relief got mixed up with heavy guilt; was it his wish that killed his hated father?

When his first wife died, the good home he managed to create fell apart and he collapsed with it. The ghost of the past started to haunt him, suggesting that his loss is a possible punishment for the hatred he felt toward his parents. The metaphor of "a computer going all wrong" reflects the unbearable sense of helplessness and fear, resulting from lack of control and reason. The feeling of being attacked by an unknown power may trigger rage and the wish to destroy. We expect a computer, like a home, to offer help and support. Thus, when it does not, when it does the opposite, it could be very frightening. When it "goes all wrong", it all falls apart and there is nothing to hold on to or trust.

As a young and able person Jim relied on himself, on his vitality and energy. The loss of his first wife was painful but also confusing. Was he somehow responsible for her death, like he felt when his father died? Was this a punishment? The toxic mix of guilt, anger, and the pain of loss was more than he could bear on his own. I believe that in a paradoxical way my failing to notice his lateness, which made him feel like he felt with his mother and second wife—not understood and neglected—allowed both of us to recognise and use a preverbal language, a communication by action. Yet, this time he was eventually heard. I was paying attention and trying to understand him. Being angry with me in the safety of therapy also created an opportunity to confront and justify anger. He was contained as he felt understood and accepted. By realising what caused the cycle of fear and destructive rage, he was able to protect his vulnerable "inner home". If we use his metaphor of the computer that went all wrong, we could say that he knows now which button to press. By understanding what went wrong, he gained enough control over his psyche.

Jim grew up in an unsafe environment in his parents' home and then the war. Feeling rejected and in danger, he was left with the task of finding and internalising a good object. He needed to free the space within him and find a way to create his own inner and outer fairy tale as well as a real home.

Conclusion

Empedocles, the ancient Greek philosopher, as presented by Kirk and Raven (1957), believed that one of the main principles of existence is the tension between love and strife (hate), between unification and separation.

Home, whether our body, an external construct, or an internal concept, provides the containment for this balance we call life. Writing this chapter, I was trying to navigate the vast ocean of meanings and emotions attached to the word "home". I know I touched only the surface. The concept of home is like a transitional object, part of the attempt to adjust to life out of the womb, where constant negotiation takes place between the wish to be held tight and the need to breathe freely. In Jim's story we saw that when, at an early age, home in the moment is experienced as frightening and unboundaried, then later on in life there is a need to clear the debris and free the space to create an internal home, good enough to be carried into the world.

Language is part of the internal home. Jim's mother tongue communicated danger and made him feel isolated and separated. My experience of German, my mother's tongue, also carried with it the notions of fear and separation. This similar aspect of our early experience of language may have contributed to Jim feeling understood. We communicated in English, yet I am a foreigner with a foreign accent. This afforded the distance that enabled Jim to negotiate the delicate balance between love and strife. He found a way of letting go, of freeing himself from the haunting past, yet not forgetting.

References

Bollnow, O. F. (1961). Lived-space. *Philosophy Today*, 5: 33.

Heaney, S., & Hughes, T. (2005). *The Rattle Bag: An Anthology of Poetry*. London: Faber & Faber.

Kirk, G. S., & Raven, J. E. (1957). *The Presocratic Philosophers*. London: Cambridge University Press.

Laplanche, J., & Pontalis, J.-B. (1988). *The Language of Psychoanalysis*. London: Karnac.

Merleau-Ponty, M. (1962). *Phenomenology of Perception*. London: Routledge.

Papadopoulos, R. K. (2002). *Therapeutic Care of Refugees: No Place Like Home*. London: Karnac.

Smith, D. L. (1991). *Hidden Conversations*. London: Routledge.

Wagner, Z. (2000). *Five Generation*. S. Wilson (Trans.). Israel: self-published.

Winnicott, D. W. (1986). *Home Is Where We Start From*. London: Pelican.

Index